Mississippi
BEAR HUNTER
Holt Collier

Mississippi BEAR HUNTER Holt Collier

GUIDING
TEDDY ROOSEVELT
AND A LIFETIME
OF ADVENTURE

MARK NEAVES

THE
History
PRESS

Published by The History Press
Charleston, SC
www.historypress.com

First published 2023

Manufactured in the United States

ISBN 9781467154581

Library of Congress Control Number: 2023937175

*This book is dedicated to my grandfather Clyde Neaves,
who loved history as much as I do. His memory lives on in his children,
grandchildren and great-grandchildren.*

CONTENTS

ACKNOWLEDGEMENTS

Writing this book has been a pleasure and an honor. I want to thank the people who have made writing this book possible. First, I want to thank my wife of twenty-two years, Marti, who is my rock. She has been patient and helpful throughout the research and writing of this book. I want to thank my wonderful children, Riley and Emma Kay, whom we love dearly. My wife and my children have always been my most ardent supporters. I don't know what I would do without them.

I am so grateful to my grandfather, Clyde Neaves, who is primarily responsible for my love of history. As a World War II veteran, he spent many hours telling me stories about his experiences fighting in the Pacific Theater and his childhood during the Great Depression. I am also thankful that my father, Lonnie, who also loves history, taught me to work hard and chase my dreams. My mother, Kay, who passed away in 1998, always believed in me and pushed me to do my best. I also want to thank my stepmother, Ann, who has always loved me like her own.

I am eternally grateful to Joe Gartrell, my editor, who has been kind, patient and helpful throughout this process. I also want to thank The History Press for making this history teacher's dream of publishing a biography of a historical figure come true.

Chapter 1

BORN INTO SLAVERY

Howell Hinds sat on his front porch, rocking slowly, a cloud of cigar smoke encircling his head as he listened to crickets chirping softly in the distance. His mind reeled with the possibilities of improving his Home Hill Plantation and establishing his new Plum Ridge Plantation, just north in Greenville, Mississippi. Suddenly, his thoughts were interrupted by the wailing of a newborn baby. The cries came from the plantation's slave quarters, just across a large green field from the "big house." The baby's angry cry signaled that Howell Hinds gained a new slave and Harrison and Daphne Collier had gained a son. Staring down at their squirming, angry baby, with his shock of curly black hair, they had no clue that the baby they named Holt was to become one of the most adventurous men Mississippi would ever produce.

The Collier family's association with the Hinds family came about when Thomas Hinds married Lemenda Green, daughter of Thomas Marston Green, in 1807. Born in Virginia in November 1723, Thomas Green served as a colonel in the Continental army during the American Revolution. After the war, Green traveled to Mississippi, settled in Jefferson County and established a large plantation. With a need for manual labor, Green began to buy slaves, putting them to work clearing the land, plowing, planting and harvesting crops. One of those slaves was Allen Collier, the future grandfather of Holt Collier. On her marriage to Thomas Hinds, Allen Collier's ownership was transferred to Lemenda Green as a wedding present from her father. Packing his meager possessions, Allen traveled to the Home

Hill Plantation and began to adjust to life at a new plantation, serving a new master. It was Thomas and Lemenda's marriage that began a relationship between the Hinds and the Colliers that lasted for over sixty years.

The Home Hill Plantation had been the brainchild of Thomas Hinds's father, John, who was born in Virginia in 1753. Feeling strongly about America's struggle for independence, John enlisted in the Continental army in 1781, achieving the rank of captain. After the war, Captain Hinds acquired properties in Virginia, Kentucky, Tennessee and Mississippi. With an adventurous spirit and hopes of becoming more prosperous, he left Virginia and settled in Jefferson County, Mississippi. A mostly undeveloped land, Mississippi was full of possibilities for those willing to work hard. Clearing his land, Captain Hinds soon turned Home Hill Plantation into profitable farmland, which would establish him as an important planter in the area. Much of the plantation's progress, unfortunately, was due to slave labor. Despite living through the American Revolution and the establishment of a plantation in the wilderness, Captain Hinds died at the age of fifty-four, four months before his son, Thomas, married Lemenda Green. At twenty-seven years old, Thomas Hinds inherited the Home Hill Plantation.

Moving into Home Hill Plantation, the newlyweds began immediately planning for their future. No longer under the long shadow of his father, Thomas began to build his reputation and quickly became one of the rising planter-aristocrats in Jefferson County. With the birth of their only son, Cameron Howell Hinds, in 1808, Thomas was elated that the Hinds family name would be carried on for another generation. As a friend of Andrew Jackson and the son-in-law of Thomas Green, Thomas Hinds's prospects seemed endless. However, Thomas's attention was soon diverted to the conflicts taking place in Europe.

Embroiled in conflict, Great Britain and France were attempting to keep the United States from trading with each other. As the United States was a young country that relied heavily on trade, its economy was shaken by the war in Europe. When James Madison, the sitting president of the United States, was informed that Napoleon Bonaparte was considering lifting the trade restrictions, Madison cut off all trade with Britain and supported France. Americans were also angry about the actions of the British Royal Navy, which was pirating American merchant ships and indenturing U.S. sailors. The United States, having been independent of Britain for less than three decades, was determined not to be bullied into submission by the British and declared war on Great Britain on June 17, 1812. The second

Andrew Jackson, the hero of the Battle of New Orleans, was a close friend of Thomas Hinds and seventh president of the United States. *Courtesy of the Library of Congress. Contributor: Ritchie, Alexander Hay-Carter, Dennis Malone.*

American war of independence had begun, and Thomas Hinds was anxious to do his part for his country.

Hinds's first foray into military action came years before the War of 1812 when, as a dragoon, he helped repulse former vice president Aaron Burr's attempt to take over parts of the Mississippi and Louisiana Territories. Burr, who had served under Thomas Jefferson as vice president and had killed Alexander Hamilton in a duel, believed he could create his own country by establishing a firm hold in the then-western part of the United States. When his efforts failed, President Thomas Jefferson attempted to prosecute Burr for treason, but Burr was eventually acquitted. The Burr Conspiracy and his part in helping to stop it only enflamed Thomas Hinds's military ambitions. Having achieved the rank of lieutenant in the territorial militia, Hinds was promoted to the rank of major in 1813. Eager to put his military experience to good use, Hinds volunteered for the War of 1812 and was placed under the command of his old friend General Andrew Jackson.

Great Britain, having helped Spain repulse Napoleonic forces in the past, requested that Spain allow British troops to garrison at Fort San Miguel, and the Spanish obliged. The British planned to assemble enough troops at Pensacola and then march to take New Orleans and conquer the city that was home to one of the most important, if not the most important, seaports in America. The British believed that if New Orleans fell into their hands, the war would be won. Andrew Jackson had other plans as he arrived in Pensacola on November 6, 1814, with four thousand American troops under his command. Jackson sent a letter to the Spanish governor, Manrique, hoping to avoid bloodshed; however, his pleas for peace fell on deaf ears. On November 7, Jackson sent his troops to attack the city. Soon after the battle started, the British were overwhelmed, and Manrique waved the white flag. When the smoke cleared, less than a dozen Americans had been killed, and the British fled to Fort San Carlos. As great a victory as the Battle of Pensacola was, the most famous battle of the War of 1812 was still on the horizon, and Thomas Hind would also take part in that battle.

On January 8, 1815, the sun had yet to rise over the Chalmette Plantation on the banks of the Mississippi River when the British army charged toward the American position. The 5,700 American troops were a motley of professional soldiers, militia, Native Americans, frontiersmen, free men of color and even a few pirates. Entrenched in the mud and hiding behind cotton bales, the American forces waited patiently until the 8,000 British soldiers came into range before opening fire. In the thick of the fighting, Major Thomas Hinds bolted across the battlefield leading his Mississippi cavalry unit into the fusillade of British fire. When the battle was over, the American forces had suffered only sixty-two casualties, while the British suffered an unbelievable 2,034. The Battle of New Orleans propelled Andrew Jackson to national fame and would play a large part in his eventual election as the seventh president of the United States. Thomas Hinds also benefited from the battle when he was promoted to the rank of brigadier general of the Mississippi territorial militia in 1815. The Battle of New Orleans would be immortalized in a song by Johnny Horton in April 1959.

Shortly after the end of the War of 1812, Mississippi became the twentieth state in the nation. In 1817, just two years after Mississippi achieved statehood, tragedy struck the Home Hill Plantation when Lemenda passed away at the age of twenty-seven. Her untimely death left Thomas a widower and their eleven-year-old son, Howell, motherless. Grief-stricken, General Hinds resigned from his military commission and entered politics. Despite giving up his military career, Thomas was seldom home, leaving young Howell in the care of Harrison and Daphne Collier. Harrison, the son of Allen Collier, had followed in his father's footsteps and was also serving as a house slave. Harrison, like Allen, proved himself trustworthy, wise and dependable, soon becoming a trusted confidant to Thomas. Under the care of Harrison and Daphne, Howell grew into a well-educated, polite southern gentleman. With such a familial relationship existing between Harrison and Daphne and the Hinds family, it comes as no surprise that Howell would later take their son, Holt, under his wing.

After serving as a successful member of the Mississippi Territorial Council in 1806, Thomas Hinds decided to run for governor of Mississippi in 1820. His opponent George Poindexter was born in Louisa County, Virginia, in 1779. Leaving Virginia, George passed the bar. Settling in Natchez, Mississippi, he started his practice, and with hard work and a little luck, his law practice began to surge. Poindexter had also served on the Mississippi Territorial General Assembly and was so successful in Mississippi becoming a state that he was dubbed the Father of Mississippi's First Constitution. The 1820 gubernatorial election ended in defeat for Thomas Hinds, as he was beaten by Poindexter in a landslide. With his hopes dashed, Hinds would once again be called back into public service by his old friend and president, Andrew Jackson.

In 1826, when the Chickasaw and the Choctaw failed to relinquish their lands east of the Mississippi River, Secretary of War James Barbour, at the insistence of President Jackson, appointed William Clark, John Coffee and Thomas Hinds as commissioners to convince the two tribes to give up their land. The proceedings, which were drawn out over several months, finally came to a head on November 1, 1826, when the tribes stated that they had no wish to give up their land to move west of the Mississippi River. The Native Americans stated that they wanted to end their negotiations by parting like brothers. This was not the answer that Clark, Hinds and Coffee had wished for; however, success finally came for other negotiators in 1830 and 1832, when the tribes signed the Treaty of Pontotoc, ceding their land to the United States government.

Not deterred by his failed negotiations with the Native Americans, Thomas decided to run for the United States Congress as a representative for Mississippi's First District. Running as a Democrat, he was elected to office and began to serve in 1827 with his term extending to 1829, as he finished out the term of the former First District congressman. Running again, he was elected to office in 1829. Between May 1828 and March 1831, he missed 56 of 351 roll call votes. During his time in Congress, Thomas left the running of Home Hill Plantation in the hands of his son, nineteen-year-old Howell Hinds. Resigning his congressional position before his term expired, he returned to Home Hill Plantation, where he lived the rest of his life out of the public eye, dying from a ruptured blood vessel in August 1840 at the age of sixty. In honor of his public and military service, the State of Mississippi immortalized him forever by naming Hinds County after him, home to Jackson, Mississippi, the state capital.

As his father's sole survivor, Howell Hinds, thirty-two, inherited the Home Hill Plantation, the slaves who worked on it and his father's finances. Despite Thomas's need to remain in the public eye, Howell was more satisfied with running the plantation, serving only one term in the Mississippi general assembly. Howell eventually increased his land and slaveholdings, investing in the former Choctaw-owned land north of Home Hill Plantation. The land he bought had been ceded to the United States by the Choctaw when they signed the Treaty of Doak's Stand. The Treaty of Doak's Stand had been negotiated by none other than Andrew Jackson and Howell's father, Thomas Hinds. During the negotiations, Jackson said to the Choctaw representatives, "If you refuse [to sign]…the nation [Choctaws] will be destroyed." Whether or not Jackson's words swayed them to act, the Choctaw chiefs signed the treaty on October 18, 1820.

Howell, who had married Drusilla "Sallie" Cocks in September 1829, threw his effort into developing his new land. With Thomas absent much of the time, Howell had taken control of the farming and slaving operations, amassing a small fortune for himself and his budding family. Their first child, Thomas Hinds, named after Howell's father, was born two days before Christmas in 1830. Unfortunately, Sallie passed away in April 1841, not having recovered from giving birth to her second child, Coleman. Before she passed away, Howell had taken serious steps toward developing the land that would come to be known as Plum Ridge Plantation.

A widower with a considerable fortune, Howell Hinds remained unmarried until Valentine's Day 1849. His new bride, a mother of four young daughters, was Mary Ann Coleman Lape of Port Gibson, Mississippi. A well-educated woman from a respectable family, Mary Ann was the widow of William Lape, a planter and merchant from Port Gibson. Mary Ann would give birth to four Hinds children, one of whom would die before her first birthday. Howell and Mary Ann's devotion to each other would last until their deaths. Between their existing children and the brood they produced together, they were blessed with many grandchildren.

Believing that Plum Ridge was "no place for women and children," Howell left his wife, sons and stepdaughters and traveled north to develop his new plantation. Taking most of his slaves to Plum Ridge Plantation, Howell left Harrison, Daphne and their children behind to help Mary Ann with the daily operations of the plantation. Arriving at Plum Ridge, Howell slaves began the difficult task of clearing the land. The work was made more difficult by the Mississippi heat, humidity, a variety of poisonous snakes, mosquitoes and the constant threat of accidental death. As much as Howell was needed at his budding plantation, his proclivities for gambling and drinking drew him to the Mississippi River.

The waters of the Mississippi River begin at Lake Itasca in Minnesota and end in the Gulf of Mexico, 2,340 miles later. The mighty river has helped shape the history of the United States by allowing people to travel, trade and even gamble on its brown, churning waters. Riverboat gambling brought a form of entertainment, excitement and obsession to many men in the mid-1800s; Howell Hinds was not immune to its pleasures. Howell, like many men of his time, would gamble on almost anything: horse racing, shooting matches, card games and dice. Howell's love for gambling and drinking is likely another reason he left his wife and children behind when he traveled to his new plantation. Plum Ridge, which was located a short distance from the Mississippi River, provided Howell with easy access to the gambling boats that traveled up and down the river. Aboard those boats, liquor flowed like water, money was lost and gained and violence often ensued. In 1835, frontier justice was doled out as five cardsharps were hanged for cheating in Mississippi.

Lake Itasca is the source of the mighty Mississippi River. *Library of Congress. Contributor: Rothstein, Arthur.*

With Howell's long absence from Home Hill Plantation, Harrison and Daphne Collier fell into a comfortable routine of helping raise Howell and Mary Ann's children, along with their own. Daphne, who was ten years younger than Howell, worked as a housekeeper, seamstress and nurse at Home Hill Plantation. Working as house slaves, Harrison's and Daphne's lives were less labor intensive than those who labored in the fields under the unforgiving Mississippi sun. When Holt was born in 1846, Daphne had already given birth to a son named Marshall. After Holt's birth, Daphne would give birth to eight more children, each of which would belong to Howell Hinds until after the Civil War.

CHAPTER 2

RAISED TO HUNT

T homas Hinds, who was named after his grandfather, took young Holt under his wing, no doubt leaving the four-year-old confused and saddened when Thomas left to attend the state college in Oxford, Mississippi, in 1850. The University of Mississippi, also known as Ole Miss, was chartered by the Mississippi state legislature on February 24, 1844, making it the first public university in the state. Four years later, Ole Miss admitted its first 80 students. Over the next seventeen years, Ole Miss's enrollment continued to grow, and in 1861, shortly after Mississippi seceded from the Union, a total of 135 students and faculty members formed the University Grays and enlisted in the Eleventh Mississippi Infantry. Engaged in heavy fighting throughout the war, the University Grays' most devastating fight came on July 3, 1863, in Gettysburg, Pennsylvania. It was during Pickett's infamous charge that the University Grays suffered a 100 percent casualty rate. When the Civil War came to an end, Ole Miss reopened its doors and has become one of the most prominent universities in the southeast, enrolling over 23,000 students in 2021.

Traveling up the Mississippi River by steamboat, Thomas disembarked at Memphis, Tennessee, and traveled on to Holly Springs, where he checked into an inn owned by Mr. Mike Epps. Howell had given Thomas $185, a great deal of money for the time, to cover his traveling expenses and his tuition. During the night, someone broke into Thomas's trunk and stole his money. Howell, not a man to be trifled with, insisted that Mr. Epps be held responsible for the lost money since the theft occurred on his property.

The famous Lyceum at the University of Mississippi. It was built in 1848 and is the oldest building at the university. *Library of Congress. Contributor: Jack Boucher.*

Refusing to take responsibility for the stolen money, Howell took Epps to court, and in October 1854, *Epps v. Hinds* was brought before the High Court of Errors and Appeals of Mississippi. The court ruled in favor of Hinds, stating that when Hinds locked his money away in his locker, he had done everything within his power to protect his money. Since the money was stolen from the hotel that Mr. Epps owned and he had not posted a disclaimer warning his guests that he wasn't responsible for stolen property, he was also liable. While at Ole Miss, Thomas spent much of his time yearning to return to Home Hill and Plum Ridge.

A veritable oasis, Home Hill Plantation sat on a hill, overlooking a large stand of oaks. The plantation was almost entirely self-sufficient, with a henhouse that provided eggs, a pasture for raising sheep and cattle and pens full of hogs that were slaughtered in the winter, salted and smoked in the plantation's smokehouse. With all these resources, people on the Hinds plantation ate well, including the slaves. No evidence or accounts exist of Howell Hinds using the whip or being cruel to his slaves, but that didn't stop some of them from attempting to escape to freedom. In October 1850, Howell placed an ad in the *Mississippi Free Trader and Natchez Gazette,* offering a reward for the return of a mulatto slave named Morgan, who stood about six feet two inches tall and weighed 175 pounds, with curly hair and gray eyes. According to eyewitnesses, Morgan boarded a steamboat headed to New Orleans. In the last line of the ad, Hinds offered a liberal reward for the return of his missing slave.

The woods surrounding the Home Hill Plantation teemed with wild game such as whitetail deer, bobwhite quail, foxes, gray squirrels, black bears and many other species. While not gambling or taking care of the farm, Howell spent much of his time in the woods, gun in hand, hoping for a successful hunt. His love of the hunt provided him with countless hours of enjoyment; it also provided his plantation with a variety of wild game for the table. Thomas and Howell, like many hunters at the time, relied on a large pack of hunting hounds to chase their prey. The care of the plantation's kennel soon fell to Marshall and Holt Collier, who had both reached an age where they could work without constant supervision. Feeding the hounds, allowing them to run and cleaning up after them developed in Holt a lifelong love for canines. After being freed from slavery, for the better part of his life, Holt would own and hunt with a large pack of hounds.

Thomas and Howell Hinds and Holt's father, Harrison, no doubt played a large part in influencing young Holt's interests and behavior. Howell and Harrison were also responsible for his lifelong dislike of alcohol. Before being taken to Plum Ridge, Holt escorted Howell Hinds and his father, Harrison, on a hunt where the two men became so intoxicated that they could not travel home for the night. Forced to camp, they built a fire and continued to drink. Whooping, hollering and howling at the moon, they scared young Holt so badly, he swore off alcohol for the rest of his life. Later, as a soldier and a professional hunting guide, he would be offered alcohol on numerous occasions, only to refuse it time and time again.

Returning home from Ole Miss, Thomas Hinds, curious to see his father's progress on their new plantation, chose ten-year-old Holt to act as his valet. Leaving his father, mother, brothers and sisters behind, Holt mounted a surrey and rode for the river. Having never seen a steamboat in his life, young Holt was awestruck by the powerful machines that churned the muddy waters of the Mississippi. Later in life, Collier gave an account of his fear of boarding the steamboat saying, "the master [Thomas] took me by the hand and led me across the plank." With none of his family traveling north to Plum Ridge, Holt felt a mixture of sadness, excitement and adventure as the steamboat pulled away from the bank and headed north. This trip, to Washington County, would be the first step toward Holt Collier's rise as a legendary hunter.

Steamboats being loaded by plank on the Mississippi River. This is the way that Holt Collier boarded a steamboat for Plum Ridge Plantation. *Library of Congress. Contributor: Detroit Publishing.*

Established in 1827, Washington County, Mississippi, was named after the father of the United States, George Washington. Long before any White men set foot in Washington County, the Native Americans had thriving communities along the banks of the mighty river. Remnants of their civilization survive in the form of the earthen Winterville Mounds. Through intensive, backbreaking labor, the Native Americans constructed each mound by first digging up the dirt, placing it in baskets, carrying it to the construction sites and then stamping it down. The Winterville Mounds are an amazing feat of construction, with twenty-three mounds that surround a centrally located mound that stands fifty-five feet in the air. It is one of the ten largest mounds in North America. Each year, tourists, anthropologists and archaeologists travel to Washington County to study the mounds.

It wasn't its history that drew White men to Washington County in the mid-1800s; it was the rich, dark alluvial soil, deposited on the banks of the Mississippi River repeatedly for thousands of years as the mighty river swelled and overflowed its banks time and time again. The soil was wonderful for growing cotton, and soon, Washington County's slave population far outnumbered its free population. According to an 1850 census, there were 7,836 slaves in the county, while the number of Whites living there was just 546. In 1850, the county had the highest value of farm property in the state but lacked a public school and was home to only two churches. Today, the county seat is Greenville, which is the largest city in the Mississippi Delta with over 30,000 residents.

The isolation of the Plum Ridge Plantation would have seemed strange and foreign to young Holt, who had become accustomed to many visitors passing through and staying at the Home Hill Plantation. One of the frequent visitors to Home Hill was the illustrious Colonel Jefferson Davis, a senator from Mississippi, future president of the Confederate States of America and close friend of Howell Hinds. Plum Ridge, on the other hand, was rustic, built on what was considered the Mississippi frontier and not fit for visitors. Disembarking at Greenville, about a mile from Plum Ridge, one traveler said of the town, "It was like landing in the wilderness."

This "wilderness" would help to mold Holt Collier into the man he would become.

As Plum Ridge continued to grow, the number of slaves living there rose until it reached fifty-eight. In contrast, other plantation owners in Washington County who farmed thousands of acres kept hundreds of slaves in bondage, toiling away from dawn till dusk to produce as much cotton as possible. Cotton was the lifeblood of Mississippi's economy, and the state produced as much as four million bales in 1860. With its incredible ability to produce cotton, Mississippi became the richest state in America. Much of Mississippi's cotton was shipped to Great Britain, where it was turned into cloth and then resold to Americans at a higher price. Due to America's lack of industrialization, Great Britain became the world's leading textile producer. Unfortunately, the cotton boom caused the number of enslaved people in Mississippi to rise from 3,489 slaves in 1800 to 436,631 in 1860.

With food less plentiful at Plum Ridge, hunting would play a large role in feeding the growing plantation. Shortly after arriving at Plum Ridge, Howell gave Holt, age ten, a shotgun and a pony, instructing him to keep the tables piled high with fresh meat. With paranoia still lingering in the South from Nat Turner's slave rebellion, many plantation owners would have shuddered at the thought of placing a weapon in the hands of a slave. Turner's Rebellion, as it became known, ended in the deaths of fifty Whites, who were killed with knives, clubs and muskets. The rebellion ended when Turner and fifty-five others were hanged by the State of Virginia. Howell's decision to allow Holt to carry a gun gives us a glimpse into how much he trusted his young slave.

Placing him on the front porch of the slave quarters, Thomas ordered Holt to kill any bird that flew within range. With birds aplenty, Holt brought down pigeons, robins, blackbirds and other species, which were promptly dressed, cooked and served to those who lived on the plantation. Birds came in such great numbers that Holt's right shoulder became so sore he had to switch to his left to continue firing. The more he practiced, the more proficient he became at shooting from both his left and right shoulders. His marksmanship improved so much that Howell Hinds allowed Holt to shoot competitively against some of the greatest wing shooters in Mississippi. Not only did Howell allow Holt to compete, but he also bet large sums of money on his young slave to win the competitions. Once, while participating in a quail shoot against well-known marksman Lomax Anderson, Holt won a $1,000 purse for Howell Hinds.

As Holt grew, so did Washington County, and Greenville soon became known as the Queen City of the Mississippi Delta, transforming itself into a popular location to board and disembark from the Mississippi River. The county's population almost doubled from 8,000 to 15,679 residents, 14,467 of them slaves. It is hard to imagine a world in which Holt did not understand that his life was very different from that of most slaves in the county. In an interview, Holt said, referring to Howell and Thomas Hinds, "They raised me; my mother stayed on the old plantation." He went on to recall how they took him to Niagara Falls, Saratoga, New York, Long Beach and other destinations. "They wouldn't hardly step foot off the front gallery 'thout I went along. When I got big, I wore finer clothes than they did," Holt said. Most of the slaves in Washington County spent most of their days working away under the hot Mississippi sun.

Proof of Thomas and Howell Hinds's preferential treatment of Holt was evident when they bought him a $215 twelve-gauge Scott shotgun. If converted into today's money, the shotgun would cost somewhere over $7,000. Putting the shotgun to good use, Howell Hinds placed Holt next to a stand of chinaberry trees and told him to shoot every blackbird he saw. Due to his expert marksmanship, it wasn't long before the whole plantation was treated to blackbird pie. Growing tired of killing small game, Holt began to practice with a rifle.

When he became a crack shot with a rifle, Thomas and Howell Hinds decided that it was time for Holt to set his sights on a larger game. The pinnacle of big game hunting in Mississippi, at the time, was the black bear.

Despite being the smallest bear in North America, black bears, which stand anywhere between four to six feet tall with the males weighing between 130 to 350 pounds, wreaked havoc on plantation foodstuffs, campsites and farm animals. They became such a problem that many plantation owners would assign a slave to sit by the pigpens all night to raise an alarm when a black bear came, hoping to dine on pork. With sharp claws, sharp teeth and the ability to run up to thirty miles per hour, the black bear can be dangerous when pushed by hunters. Hunting in thick canebrakes, not all hunters who came face-to-face with black bears lived to tell the tale.

With experienced hunters such as Howell and Thomas Hinds, Holt was in good hands as they eased through the foliage around Plum Ridge, keeping their eyes open, listening for the bay of their hounds. Finally, the hounds let out their long, loud bay, meaning they were on the scent of a bear. Crashing through the underbrush and the canebrake, they saw a black bear trying to fight off the angry pack of dogs. Taking careful aim, Holt squeezed the trigger, dropping the bear to the ground. At ten years old, he had killed his first bear. Throughout his lifetime, he would kill over three thousand black bears, more than Davey Crockett and Daniel Boone combined, solidifying his place in the annals of hunting greats.

CHAPTER 3

OFF TO WAR

W ith Holt on the prowl, gun in hand, the plantation enjoyed fresh bear meat, venison, possum, barbecued raccoon and blackbird pie. As Holt was waging war on any wild game that moved or flew through the canebrakes, trouble was brewing throughout the southern states. With the success of Harriet Beecher Stowe's book *Uncle Tom's Cabin*, trouble began in earnest between the North and the South. Stowe's vivid portrayal of the angry, abusive slaveholder Simon Legree, who chose greed over humanity, opened many northerners' eyes to what could happen if a person like Legree owned slaves. The South believed that its right to own slaves fell under the Tenth Amendment. The Tenth Amendment states that the federal government has only those powers mentioned in the Constitution and that the rights not mentioned fall to the people of the United States and the states themselves. Southerners viewed slavery as a right that fell to the states and, as such, could not be revoked or infringed on by the federal government.

The presidential election of 1860 was unusual in that it had four strong candidates vying for America's highest office. The four candidates were Republican Abraham Lincoln, Democrat John C. Breckinridge, Constitutional Union Party candidate John Bell and Democrat Stephen Douglas. Most of the southern states voted for Stephen Douglas, but due to those states' low populations, he received only 19 electoral votes. John Bell received just 39 electoral votes, John C. Breckinridge received 72 electoral votes and Abraham Lincoln won a decisive victory with 180

President Abraham Lincoln guided the United States through the carnage of the Civil War. He was assassinated by John Wilkes Booth at Ford's Theater. *Library of Congress. Contributor: Alexander Gardner.*

electoral votes. As a Republican, Abraham Lincoln was the most despised candidate in the southern states; his name was intentionally left off ballots throughout the South.

The Republican Party, which was formed on March 20, 1854, wanted to keep slavery from spreading to the territories but had no real opposition to keeping slavery in the states and territories where it already existed. However, the South viewed the Republican Party's ideologies as a doorway to full emancipation and equality for African Americans.

If the election of 1860 was the powder keg, Lincoln's election was the spark that caused it to explode. Even before the election, South Carolina had chosen a convention that was determined to secede if Lincoln was elected president. True to its word, South Carolina seceded from the Union on December 20, 1860, followed by Mississippi, Florida, Alabama, Georgia, Louisiana, Texas, Virginia, Arkansas, North Carolina and Tennessee. The next step taken by the seceded states happened on February 4, 1861, when they sent delegates to Montgomery, Alabama, to form what would become known as the Confederate States of America. The delegates elected Mississippi senator and close friend of Howell Hinds Jefferson Davis as the new president of the Confederacy. A graduate of the West Point Military Academy, Davis had been instrumental in his roles as a Mississippi and a federal government official. Having refused to attend the convention in Montgomery, Davis was pruning roses at his home in Mississippi when he was informed that he had been elected president of the Confederate States of America.

With a mixture of emotions, Davis traveled to Montgomery and was sworn in as the president of the Confederate States of America on February 18, 1861. Standing on the steps of the Alabama state capitol in Montgomery, worry raced through his mind. Fearful of what lay ahead, Davis said, "Upon my weary heart was showered smiles, plaudits, and flowers, but beyond them, I saw troubles and thorns innumerable." Today, the spot where he took his oath of office is marked by a full-sized bronze star. In his inauguration speech, Davis laid the blame at the feet of the northern states when he said, "Through many years of controversy, with our late associates, the Northern States, we have vainly endeavored to secure tranquility and to obtain respect for the right to which we are entitled." It was clear that Davis was determined to lead the newly formed government into an era of independence, which would allow the southern sates much more autonomy than they were given under the United States Constitution.

As tensions between the North and the South continued to grow, the northern army abandoned all federally held forts in the South, except for Fort Sumter, which is located on the coast of South Carolina. The fort was under the command of Major Robert Anderson, a veteran of the Mexican-American War who had been appointed commander of Fort Sumter by General Winfield Scott himself. General Scott, known as "Old Fuss and Feathers," was the highest-ranking Union general at the beginning of the war. The Confederate troops, commanded by Brigadier General P.G.T. Beauregard, had orders to force the Union troops to surrender the crucial fort. In a letter to Anderson on April 11, 1861, Beauregard wrote, "I am ordered by the government of the Confederate States to demand the evacuation of Fort Sumter." He also wrote, "The flag which you have upheld so long and with much fortitude, under the most trying circumstances, may be saluted by you on taking it down." Robert Anderson replied that his sense of honor and obligation to his government would not allow him to evacuate the fort. With neither side willing to negotiate, the

Left: General P.G.T Beauregard, commander at Fort Sumter. He would also take over command at the Battle of Shiloh following the death of Albert Sydney Johnston. *Library of Congress.*

Right: The Civil War reenactment group based on the real Turner's Battery, First Mississippi Light Artillery. *Courtesy of Mark Neaves.*

first shots of the Civil War were fired on April 12, 1861. Running low on resources, Major Robert Anderson had no choice but to surrender after thirty-six hours of being bombarded by Confederate mortar and artillery fire. The only casualty came when a round prematurely exploded during a one-hundred-gun salute, killing Private Daniel Hough and wounding another soldier.

On hearing that Lincoln had called for seventy-five thousand military volunteers, even before the first shots at Fort Sumter were fired, Confederate president Jefferson Davis called for one hundred thousand southerners to volunteer for military service, and they answered the call. While many plantation owners contributed to the war by providing the southern forces with monetary contributions, cotton and horses, others like Thomas and Howell Hinds signed up for the Confederate army. Howell, who was spending most of his time at the Home Hill Plantation in Jefferson County, volunteered for the Jefferson Flying Artillery. Originally organized as a cavalry unit on May 6, 1861, the unit was converted to an artillery unit when it was mustered into Confederate state service on April 1, 1861. Led by Captains William L. Harper and Putnam Darden, the battery appointed Howell Hinds as one of its two first lieutenants.

North in Washington County, Thomas Hinds, filled with Confederate fervor, volunteered for Byrne's Artillery Battery. The battery was named after its founder Ed Byrnes, a Kentuckian living near Greenville, Mississippi, who formed the battery shortly after Mississippi seceded from the Union. The citizens of Washington County, eager to do their part, quickly helped fund the battery. With funding in hand, Captain Byrnes traveled to Memphis, where he contracted Quinby & Robinson to manufacture two twelve-pound Howitzers and four six-pounders. The next step was to appoint officers, and Thomas Hind, like his father, was soon appointed to the position of lieutenant.

When the Hinds women visited Plum Ridge, Thomas and Howell returned home for one last farewell before heading to the front lines. At fourteen, Holt craved adventure, and watching men march and drill at Plum Ridge and nearby Greenville only increased his desire to join the military. Of course, with the Confederates being opposed to Black soldiers, he could never aspire to be more than a servant during the war, or so he thought. Hoping to follow his masters to war, Holt said many years later, "I begged [Thomas and Howell Hinds] like a dog, but they stuck to it—'You are too young.'" Heartbroken, he watched them ride away to Old Greenville to board a steamboat headed for Memphis. Never having defied his masters before, Holt waited till dark, gathered a few possessions and slipped away from Plum Ridge toward Old Greenville. With no moon visible, the night was pitch black, but Holt knew the woods between Plum Ridge and Old Greenville like the back of his hand.

Arriving at Old Greenville, Holt was pleased to see seven steamboats waiting to take the Confederate troops north. With no intention of being left behind, he loitered around a store belonging to Mr. Ross, a Jewish merchant, before stowing away on a steamboat named the *Vernon*. Hiding in the kitchen, Holt was surprised and fearful when he came face-to-face with one of the steamboat workers. The man could have sounded the alarm, but after listening to the young slave's story, he decided to let him stow away. Holt said of the experience, "He hid me during the trip and told me when to

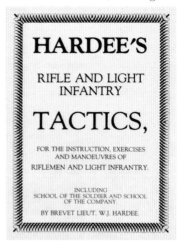

Hardee's Tactics was one of the most studied and used military tactical guides during the war. *Courtesy of openlibrary.org*

get off at Memphis." With the coast clear, Holt disembarked at Memphis, happy to have made it so far on his own.

When Thomas caught sight of young Holt, he called out to his father, who was engaged in a conversation with several officers who went on to achieve prominent positions within the Confederate army. "If we are going to hell, we'll have to take that boy," Howell said, laughing.

The officers asked Holt, "Don't you know you are going to the graveyard?"

Holt's reply was, "I got as good a chance as you."

The officers were amused by the boy's determination, but his logic couldn't be faulted. You see, a bullet has no brains, sees no color and is not concerned with who it kills; so, in that sense, young Holt was correct.

Realizing how determined Holt was, Howell gave no further protests about his young slave accompanying him to war. Luckily for Howell and Thomas, despite being in different artillery batteries, they found themselves in the same field unit. Being in the same unit meant that father and son would train and fight together under General Hardee's command. William Joseph Hardee had been a successful officer in the United States military before the War Between the States. When his home state of Georgia seceded from the Union, he resigned from his position with the U.S. military, and he was appointed brigadier general in June 1861. Fewer than five months following his appointment, he was promoted to major general. He also used his knowledge and talent to write an infantry tactic book titled *Rifle and Light Infantry Tactics*, which would come to be known as *Hardee's Tactics*. His book became one of the most widely used tactical books during the war. Under Hardee's command, Holt would serve as both Howell's and Thomas's servant, at least until he proved himself in the heat of battle.

CHAPTER 4

THE BATTLE OF SHILOH AND THE DEATH OF ALBERT SYDNEY JOHNSTON

On June 17, 1861, Nashville, Tennessee, erupted in cannon fire as its citizens hoisted the Confederate flag high above the state capital. The celebration was confirmation of the state's secession, which had happened on April 17. The citizens of Tennessee were adamant about their participation in helping to defend their state. No person was more adamant than Tennessee's own governor, Isham G. Harris, in a message to Abraham Lincoln, which stated, "Tennessee will not furnish a single man for purposes of coercion, but 50,000 if necessary for the defense of our rights and those of our Southern brothers." The governor's statement was clear: Tennessee would do whatever was necessary to defend its borders, especially Nashville.

The Confederacy's commitment to defend Nashville was quickly put to the test. General Hardee's orders to march to Virginia were abandoned, and his troops were directed to set up a line of defense between Nashville and the growing mass of Union troops gathering in Kentucky. In February, Hardee's troops, along with others, formed a snakelike, 430-mile defensive line from the Cumberland Gap in Tennessee to Missouri. Among the bustling camps, Holt worked as a personal servant, moving back and forth between artillery batteries, depending on whether Thomas or Howell required his services that day. Happy to serve the men he considered family, Holt was also anxious to be part of the action, and he didn't have to wait long for the opportunity.

As Holt was tending to a wounded man named Dunbar, a skirmish broke out near Green River Bridge. Left to his own devices, Holt grabbed a musket and ammunition and ran toward the fight. Taking careful aim, it wasn't long before Holt proved himself not only a great servant but also a deadly soldier.

Years later, during an interview, Holt recalled his part in the skirmish that would end his time as a servant and transform him into an unofficial soldier in the Confederate army.

When the fight broke out that time, they all went away and left me in camp by myself and I was a mighty little darky. Somebody had left a musket an' a sack full of cartridges. So I jes' buckled on the cartridge belt, an followed along 'till I got to where the shootin' was goin' on. All the man was a-pluggin away, so I got to a place where I could see real good an' commenced to a-shootin, too.

Twarn't long until I heard some one bust out in a big laugh behine me, and there was Mr. Tom Hinds a-settin' up might straight on his hoss.

"Look here boy, ain't you scared you'll git kilt?" Mr. Tom said, an' he looked so peculiar I couldn't help but laugh.

With his usual wit, Holt replied, "Dunno, sir: ain't my chances mighty nigh as good as yours?"

Holt, happy to be part of the action, kept pouring fire into the advancing Yankees. It was there, outside of Nashville, that he proved his willingness to kill or die for what he considered his country, regardless of his status as a slave. Later, Howell gifted young Holt a gray gelding named Medock, whom he rode for the rest of the war. After his first fight, Holt was also outfitted with a Confederate gray uniform and a shell jacket with braided edges. One can only wonder what strange looks Holt garnered from the White Confederates as he rode by them. Having "seen the elephant," a term used to describe a soldier's first time seeing battle, Holt was ready for even more action. Unbelievably, Holt went on to see more action and fight more valiantly than both Howell and Thomas Hinds.

While there had been several major battles and skirmishes fought since the firing on Fort Sumter, neither side had an inkling about the sheer devastation that the Civil War could produce until after the Battle of Shiloh in 1862. With the Union troops massing under the command of General Ulysses S. Grant at Pittsburg Landing, just twenty-five miles from Corinth, Mississippi, General Albert Sydney Johnston decided to go on the offensive and attack Grant's forty-two-thousand-man army before it could be reinforced by Don Carlos Buell, who commanded twenty thousand soldiers. Having won two major battles along the Tennessee River at Fort Henry and Fort Donelson, Grant planned to build on his success by marching on and taking Corinth, which was known as the Crossroads of the Confederacy.

A vital rail center, located in northeast Mississippi, Corinth was the location where the Memphis & Charleston, which ran east and west, and the Mobile & Ohio Railroad, which ran north and south, crossed. These railroads provided the Confederacy with a vital lifeline for troop and ordnance transportation. One Confederate general stated about Corinth, "If defeated here, we lose the Mississippi Valley and probably our cause." With such importance placed on the town and its railroads, General Johnston could not allow the town of over 1,500 to fall into the hands of the Union. Hoping to stop Grant before he received reinforcements from Buell, Johnston ordered his troops to march to Pittsburg Landing on April 3, 1862, but the Confederates were delayed by heavy rains. Stopping four miles from Pittsburg Landing, Johnston and his troops hunkered down for the night to prepare for the battle. The Union and Confederate troops were so close that their pickets exchanged fire throughout the night.

The next morning, most of the Union troops, unaware that their enemies were bearing down on them with deadly intent, rose from their bedrolls and began cooking breakfast. At seven o'clock, the Union soldiers' blood ran cold when they heard the "rebel yell" and saw Confederate soldiers pouring out of the woods. Shocked, Union soldiers grabbed their weapons and ran, leaving their breakfast cooking in the pan. Hungry and tired from the march, many of the Confederate soldiers stopped and began to eat the rations intended for their enemies. Some Confederates, overwhelmed by excitement, began to pillage and loot the Union camp until they saw General Johnston atop his bay thoroughbred named Fire-Eater. Laying his eyes on a green lieutenant who had stopped to pillage, General Johnston shouted, "None of that sir, we are not here for plunder." Concerned that he had embarrassed the young officer, Johnston picked up a tin cup and said, "Let this be my share of the spoils today." The cup would remain with him for what little time he had left.

When the fighting began, General Grant was upriver in Savannah, Tennessee, at Cherry Mansion, his temporary headquarters. He had just sat down for breakfast when he heard the unmistakable rumble of artillery. A cup of coffee in hand, which he never drank, Grant sprang into action, boarded his steamboat *Tigress* and was traveling full steam ahead in a matter of minutes toward Pittsburg Landing, his mind reeling. Meanwhile, around

General Albert Sydney Johnston was killed at the Battle of Shiloh. Holt Collier witnessed him being taken from the field. *Library of Congress.*

the Shiloh Methodist Church, after which the battle would eventually be named, chaos reigned as the Confederate troops pushed the Union lines further and further back. Ironically, Shiloh, which is a Hebrew word, means "peaceful one." The Battle of Shiloh was anything but peaceful.

Around two o'clock in the afternoon, at Sarah Bell's Peach Orchard, Holt Collier stood in the shade of an oak tree, preparing for the Confederates' fourth charge across the large field that separated the two armies. Exhausted and nervous, one end of the Confederate line stalled when the orders were given to move forward. Spurring Fire-Eater to the front, General Johnston used his tin cup, from earlier in the day, to tap his men's bayonets as he rode up and down the line. "These will have to do the work, men. Follow me!" he said, whirling on Fire-Eater to lead the charge.

With both sides laying down a fusillade of fire, General Johnston was struck in the back of the right leg. Having suffered nerve damage in his right leg from a wound he sustained during a duel, Johnston was not fully aware that the bullet had clipped his popliteal artery until his boot began to fill with blood. One of Johnston's staff members, governor of Tennessee Isham Harris, noticing that the general was pale and slumping in his saddle, asked, "General, are you wounded?" Swaying in his saddle, Johnston, who was barely conscious, replied, "Yes, and I fear seriously."

In an interview years later, Holt gave an eyewitness account of Johnston's death at the Peach Orchard. "A bullet struck him in the thigh, severing an artery. Six soldiers carried him to the shade of a tree where he died a short while later."

After Johnston's death, Holt says, "We run smack over the Yankees and drove 'em into the river, took their encampment, and captured everything. But after Gen'l Beauregard was put in command…he laid over Sunday to fight on Monday. Monday, they had, I think, thirty thousand reinforcements on us, and tore the army all to pieces."

Holt's estimate of the Yankee's reinforcements was wrong by about five thousand soldiers, but the result was still the same, as General Beauregard called the fighting off for the night, allowing Don Carlos Buell's twenty-five fresh troops to steam in along the Tennessee River. Day two of the fighting, April 7, would differ for the Confederacy as the Union took the offensive when Grant launched an attack at around six o'clock in the morning. With the USS *Tyler* and the USS *Lexington* docked at Pittsburg Landing, the ships launched a deadly artillery barrage in support of Grant's left flank. Outnumbered and exhausted, the Confederate army was forced to fall back. With victory snatched from their grasp, General Beauregard ordered a retreat, and the Confederate army, licking their wounds, marched twenty-five miles back to Corinth. What looked like a Confederate victory on day one had become the Confederacy's worst defeat of the war up until that point. There at Shiloh, names such as the Bloody Pond, the Hornet's Nest,

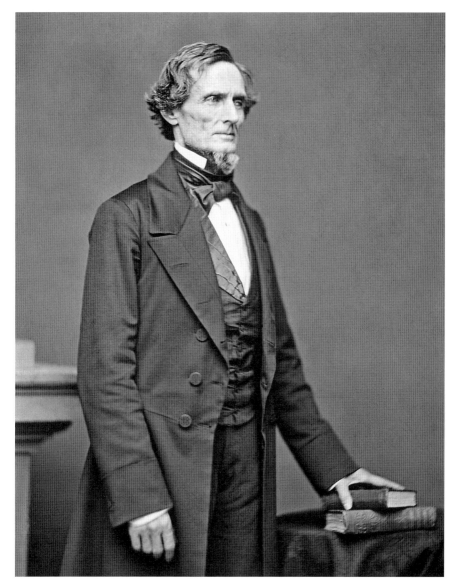

The only Confederate president of the United States, Jefferson Davis, was devastated by the loss of his friend Albert Sydney Johnston. *Library of Congress. Photograph by Matthew Brady.*

the Peach Orchard and others would become infamously associated with the death and destruction that took place there.

The death of Albert Sydney Johnston was particularly hard on Confederate president Jefferson Davis, who wrote after the war, "When Sidney Johnston fell, it was the turning point of our fate; for we had no other hand to take up his work in the West." The death of Johnston, the highest-ranking officer killed in the war, and the casualty rate of the battle were shocking to both the North and the South. During the two days of fighting, there were an estimated 23,746 casualties. With corpses scattered across the battlefields, some morbidly decorated with peach blossoms from Sarah Bell's Orchard, General Grant said, "It would have been possible to walk across the clearing in any direction stepping on dead bodies without a foot touching the ground." The battle was costly for both sides, but it doomed the South's military initiative in the Western Theater.

Their spirits broken, the Confederate troops loaded their wounded onto wagons and made their way through the muck and mire toward Corinth. At Corinth, the Tishomingo Hotel became a makeshift hospital whose walls were permeated with the screams of wounded men. Arms and legs were piled in the street outside the hotel as doctors fought the spread of infection by removing damaged limbs with a medical handsaw. Death, decay and sadness hung over the town like black storm clouds. After Shiloh, Thomas Hinds never returned to action. In a letter to General Breckenridge at the end of April 1862, Holt stated, "I am suffering and unfit for duty." Breckenridge granted him a leave of absence, from which he never returned. Wielding his enormous influence and money, Thomas used his physician's letters to become a deserter with no consequences. Holt, on the other hand, was far from finished with the war—or the war with him.

CHAPTER 5

THE CAVALRY LIFE FOR HOLT

During the Civil War, there were three distinct branches of the service: infantry, artillery and cavalry. The Confederacy identified their branches, when they could afford it, by sewing brightly colored collars and cuffs on their shell jackets. Red stood for artillery, which was divided into two categories: light and heavy artillery. As much a psychological weapon as a physical one, artillery rained down death from above with shell and shot, ripping flesh asunder with devastating effect in many battles. The Confederate artillery at the Battle of Fredericksburg was especially effective in the Confederate victory. Colonel Porter Alexander, chief of artillery under General James Longstreet's command, stated about their artillery position before the Battle of Fredericksburg, "We will comb it as if with a fine-tooth comb. A chicken could not live on that field when we open fire." The Union artillery would prove even more deadly at the Battle of Gettysburg when Pickett's troops were demolished by cannon fire.

The infantry, to which Holt Collier had gravitated at the start of the war, was represented by a blue collar and blue cuffs. The men in the infantry relied on two things: their feet and their gun. Marching for miles a day, they carried haversacks filled with personal items, a bedroll, a cartridge belt and a gun, often weighing between thirty and eighty pounds. Charging into the fray, infantry soldiers were often the first to die and sustained the heaviest casualties throughout the war. Overall, the Confederate casualty rate was worse than the Union's, with 150 out of every 1,000 Confederates killed or wounded in battle. The Union's casualty rate was much lower, with 112 out of every 1,000 soldiers killed or wounded in battle. One of the items that infantry soldiers desired the most was a good pair of shoes. Brogans, full leather shoes with pegged soles, were used by both Union and Confederate soldiers during the war. Many Confederate soldiers, toward the end of the war, had no shoes at all and were forced to march and fight barefoot.

Cavalry units wore yellow collars with yellow cuffs. On horseback, they were armed with pistols, carbines and sabers. Their ability to move fast, flank the enemy, gather information and attack quickly was vital to both the Confederate and Union forces. Nathan Bedford Forrest, the most famous cavalry soldier of the war, was known as the Devil on Horseback and the Wizard of the Saddle by both those who loved and feared him. The cavalry's mobility was demonstrated in the skirmish at Parker's Crossroads in Henderson County, Tennessee, on December 31, 1862. Attempting to withdraw across the Tennessee River, Forrest and his troops were attacked by Union troops led by Colonel Cyrus L. Dunham and Colonel John W. Fuller. Much to Forrest's surprise, he quickly found himself surrounded. Thinking quickly, Forrest yelled, "Charge them from both ways!" Luckily for Forrest and his men, being on horseback, they were able to turn the tables on the Union troops and escape with what they considered a victory.

Out of the three branches, it was the cavalry that appealed to Holt the most after the Battle of Shiloh. Growing up at the Plum Ridge Plantation, he had been trained to ride, groom horses and even break horses under the guidance of Thomas and Howell Hinds. His early education developed into a lifelong love of horses, which he would continue to ride for as long as he could sit in a saddle. Whether chasing bears through the canebrakes or Union soldiers through the thickly wooded forests of the South, Holt cut a commanding presence astride a horse. Following the battle of Shiloh, with the Confederates encamped at Corinth, the young slave/Confederate soldier encountered the Ninth Texas Cavalry. His encounter with the group of young Texans would change his life throughout the war.

The Ninth Texas Cavalry Unit was organized in October 1861 in northeast Texas. The regiment's first combat experience happened in the disputed Indian Territory when they fought at the Battles of Round Mountain and Bird Creek. Shortly after, the unit was on the move, traveling east to Arkansas in 1862. In March 1862, the Ninth Texas Cavalry proved their bravery when they participated in the Battle of Pea Ridge. The battle ended when the Confederate army fled, leaving Missouri's border

Dudley William Jones was an officer in the Ninth Texas Cavalry. *Courtesy of DeGolyer Library, Central University Libraries, Southern Methodist University.*

firmly under the control of the Union forces. After the battle, much to their dislike, the Ninth Texas Cavalry was dismounted and sent to Corinth, Mississippi. It was at Corinth that the Ninth Texas Cavalry would change young Holt's life forever.

The young soldiers of Company I, Ninth Texas Cavalry, were brash, cocky and quicker to fight than most Confederates. Together, they believed there was not an army they couldn't lick or a problem they couldn't solve. Holt Collier, also brash and daring, felt at home among these young men, whose greatest possessions were their horses. Armed to the teeth, the Titus Grays carried multiple pistols, a musket, a double-barreled shotgun and a Bowie knife. Multiple weapons allowed cavalrymen the ability to fire many times without having to pause to reload. An experienced infantryman could load and fire his weapon an average of three times a minute at a range of five hundred yards. Reloading a muzzle-loading weapon sitting on the back of a horse proved much harder.

Not only did the Titus Grays' arsenal of weapons appeal to Holt, but the way they dressed also influenced him for the rest of his life. Wearing a wide-brimmed hat turned up in the front, a pair of boots with a knee flap to protect their knees while riding through thick underbrush, a uniform made from light material and a jacket with a blue stripe on each shoulder, the

Titus Grays cut commanding figures on horseback. In 1907, at the age of sixty-one, Holt was photographed on horseback, his hounds surrounding him, dressed much the way he had been while fighting with the Titus Grays. Entrenched at Corinth, Holt and the Titus Grays had plenty of time to become acquainted as they awaited their next orders.

Under the command of General P.G.T. Beauregard, the Confederate forces at Corinth had dug heavy trenches around the town and were waiting for the approach of Major General Henry Halleck and his 125,000 Union troops in the fall of 1862. Over thirty days, Halleck and his army, which was stretched out along a ten-mile front, crept slowly toward Corinth from Pittsburg Landing. While awaiting Halleck, mounted once again, Holt and the Titus Grays became the eyes and ears of the Confederate forces at Corinth. As the Union troops drew closer, the two sides engaged in skirmishes at Booneville, Iuka, Farmington and Sharp's Mill. When Halleck came within ten miles of Corinth, the Confederate troops began to engage the much larger Union force at different points on the Union line. One soldier, stationed at Corinth, wrote to his wife, "I can sit now in my tent and hear the drums & voices in the enemy lines, which cannot be more than two miles distant. We have…killed and wounded every day.… The Yanks are evidently making heavy preparation for the attack which cannot, I think, be postponed many days longer.…Everything betokens an early engagement so make it be, for I am more than anxious that it shall come without further delay."

On May 25, Union forces stopped several thousand yards from the Confederate trenches and began raining down artillery fire on the Confederate position. Inside Corinth, twenty thousand of General Beauregard's sixty-five thousand troops were either wounded or suffering from dysentery or typhoid fever. Beauregard, who was concerned that if the Union saw his troops evacuating the town, they would advance quickly on Corinth, crushing his troops, engaged in one of the cleverest deceptions of the war. On May 29, he ordered the wounded and sick to be evacuated from Corinth via the railroads. Ordering his men to cheer loudly when empty train cars arrived, Beauregard hoped that the Union troops would assume the town was being reinforced by fresh Confederate troops. He also ordered a few soldiers to "desert" Corinth for the Union line. The "deserters," when questioned, lied, telling the Union soldiers that the Confederate army was ready to launch a major offensive on the Union position. Their lies caused General Halleck, who was overly cautious, to stall his movements toward Corinth. As more Confederates left Corinth

The Tishomingo Hotel in Corinth, Mississippi, became a makeshift hospital for the Confederate wounded after the Battle of Shiloh. *Courtesy of New York Public Library.*

in secret, Beauregard had men light fires up and down the front to give the illusion that the camp was fully occupied. The Confederate forces also placed quaker guns, logs painted black to look like cannons, along the front of their lines. From a distance, quaker guns were almost impossible to differentiate from actual artillery pieces. Finally, Halleck and his army marched into Corinth on May 29, shocked to find the town abandoned by the Confederate forces.

Meanwhile, Howell Hinds was still attempting to do his part for the war effort when he wrote to Jefferson Davis asking permission to raise a regiment of artillery. Taking advantage of his friendship with Davis, Howell returned home and began to recruit men for what he hoped would be a fully working regiment within a matter of months. However, he was disappointed when his efforts mustered only a measly eight recruits. His friendship with the president of the Confederate States paid off when he was appointed provost marshal for Jefferson County. Like his son, Thomas, Howell never returned to the battlefield, while Holt would not leave the battlefield for the remainder of the war.

Having impressed the Titus Grays with his ability to ride a horse and his superior marksmanship, Holt hoped to join the troop of wild, hard-fighting Texans. Uncharacteristically for a slave, Holt was told by his master, Howell Hinds, that he could choose to return to the plantation or fight with the Titus Grays. Holt chose to fight with the brash young cowboys. Years later, Holt described his decision to fight by saying,

> *They enrolled me jes' like they did the white men. Gen'l Forrest* [Nathan Bedford Forrest] *wanted me, and Cap'n Perry Evans from Texas, wanted me. Both of 'em went to Cunnel Howell Hinds, and he said "All right; I tried to leave the boy at home, but he wouldn't stay." The Cunnel give me one of the thoroughbreds to ride and I went in for a soldier. I went with the Texas soldiers, Gen'l Ross' Brigade, Cunnel Dudley Jones' regiment. Cap'n Perry Evan was the cap'n. I was the only colored man in the whole entire regiment that was a sho'-nuff soldier. All my white friends was good to me. I was a boy, but I was a fine shot and a fine rider. The company used to practice a heap shootin' and ridin'.*

His treatment as an equal by the White soldiers stood in stark contrast to how most other African Americans, slaves or freedmen, were treated during this period. Judged by his ability to ride, shoot, scout and hunt, he was in control of his destiny, at least for the time being.

CHAPTER 6

INTO THE FRAY

B orn in Virginia in 1809, Sterling Price was a Mexican War veteran and the governor of Missouri from 1853 to 1857. Despite viewing slavery as an evil institution, Price joined the Confederate army out of fear that the Union would use force on his beloved Missouri. As a major general, Price was under the supervision of Braxton Bragg, who ordered Price and his troops to march on Iuka, Mississippi, on September 14, 1862. At around four o'clock in the afternoon, the first shots of the Battle of Iuka were fired, and Holt Collier and the Titus Grays were in the thick of the fighting. The battle was called off at dusk with both sides retiring to their lines for the night. Confederate troops withdrew the next day, leaving Iuka in the hands of the Union. Because of the overgrown terrain and a Confederate rearguard, the Union army failed to crush Price's forces, allowing him to join forces with Major General Earl Van Dorn.

With time to lick their wounds and reconsider the loss of Corinth, Mississippi, the Confederacy was determined to recapture the important railway town. Ordered by Ulysses S. Grant to hold Corinth, Rosecrans had fifteen thousand troops in the town with eight thousand others at nearby garrisons. With a numerical advantage of three to two over Confederate general Earl Van Dorn, Rosecrans was confident that he could hold the town. Van Dorn decided to employ the element of surprise and moved his troops to Ripley, Mississippi, where he joined forces with Price. Marching toward Pocahontas, Mississippi, the combined forces threatened the Union garrison at Bolivar. Grant saw through their feint and told Rosecrans to concentrate on amassing his troops at Corinth to prepare for a Confederate attack. Unbeknownst to Van Dorn, his spy Amelia Burton had sent him a letter, which was intercepted by the Union forces, copied and sent on to Van Dorn. Burton's letter stated that the Union line was the weakest and least fortified on the northwest side of town. Immediately on reading Burton's letter, Rosecrans began to fortify the northwest side of town, preparing for the upcoming attack.

On October 2, Holt Collier and the Ninth Texas Cavalry engaged in a skirmish with Union troops who were patrolling on the outskirts of Corinth. The battle itself did not begin in earnest until the next day, when Van Dorn sent his concentrated troops, including the Ninth Texas Cavalry Company I, charging toward the Union lines. It must have been quite a shock for the Union troops to witness a Black Confederate soldier charging toward their position. Most Blacks who were part of the Confederate army were employed as cooks, servants or manual laborers. As the fighting went on, the Ninth Texas Cavalry and Holt witnessed atrocities that only a person who has been engaged in war can fully fathom. The Confederates pushed the Union forces back almost two miles before General Van Dorn called a halt to the fighting for the day. With temperatures soaring around ninety degrees, fatigue, thirst and pure exhaustion had set in for both sides.

With the fighting called off for the night, Holt and the other Titus Grays began to gather Union haversacks and dine on the spoils of war. Soldiers in both Union and Confederate camps found sleep elusive, understanding that the next day, October 4, might be their last. Before the sun had a chance to break above the trees, Confederate artillery began to rain death down on the Union lines, shaking the ground beneath them. It seemed like a great start for the Confederates, but delays were the order of the day as their advance was slowed till about nine o'clock in the morning, when the Confederates launched a vicious attack on the Union position. Once again, Holt and the Titus Grays were in the center of the charge. A soldier from Alabama described the scene like this,

> The whole of Corinth with its enormous fortifications, burst upon our view. The United States flag was floating over the forts and in the town. We were met by a perfect storm of grape[shot], canister, cannon balls, and Minie balls. Oh God! I have never seen the like! The men fell like grass.

The Union repulsed the Confederate charges four times before the Union attached bayonets and charged. The Confederates, who had been demoralized already by cannon fire and whose losses were grievous, signaled for a retreat. Confederate casualties numbered 4,848; the Union fared much better, with only 2,360 casualties.

After the Battle of Corinth and other engagements, the Ninth Texas Cavalry and Holt ended up at Abbeville, Mississippi, working as a mounted police force. In Abbeville, they witnessed the discontent of President Jefferson Davis with General Van Dorn's failures when Davis promoted General John C. Pemberton to the position of senior officer over Van Dorn. Not only was he passed over for a promotion, but General Van Dorn was also put on trial for neglect of duty on November 15, 1862. If found guilty, Van Dorn faced a court-martial, which would end his military career. After an intense trial, Van Dorn was found not guilty and placed in command of the Army of the Mississippi's cavalry. Eager to restore his good reputation, Van Dorn would not have to wait long to prove himself.

On December 20, 1862, the breath of Confederate soldiers and horses alike blossomed into small white clouds in the cold morning air as they waited for the order to attack the town of Holly Springs, Mississippi. Earlier in the year, the Union had captured the town, and General Grant began using it as a staging area to store supplies for his planned march and attack on Jackson, Mississippi. If the Confederates captured the town, they would cripple Grant's objective, keeping the state's capital safe, at least for a little while. As the sun rose above the trees, spreading its light across the town, Major General Van Dorn ordered his men to attack. Spurring their horses onward, 3,500 cavalrymen descended on Holly Springs.

Riding at the center of the line, the Ninth Texas Cavalry charged into the town, taking residents, Union soldiers and visitors by surprise. In an eight-page letter to his wife, Lucius B. Wing of Newark, Ohio, a businessman visiting Holly Springs, described his surprise when he was awakened by the sound of gunfire and the thunder of hooves. Rushing to the window, he saw the streets overrun by rebels. As the rebels entered the house, Wing said, "Good morning gentleman [*sic*], you favor us with rather an early call this morning." After being questioned he and the other occupants of the hotel were led outside of town, unharmed. Shocked by the attack, Union soldiers fled en masse. The town of Holly Springs had fallen back into the hands of the Confederacy.

At the end of the battle, Van Dorn and his forces had captured around 1,500 Union soldiers and destroyed over $1.5 million in supplies and buildings. The battle was a crushing blow for the Union forces, who were counting on those supplies. The defeat also pushed the Union army back toward Memphis, even further from its objective of Jackson, Mississippi. Grant, in his memoirs, writes about the aftermath of Holly Springs:

They came with broad smiles on their faces indicating intense joy, to ask what I was going to do now without any for my soldiers to eat. I told them I was not disturbed; that I had already sent troops and wagons to collect all the food and forage they could find fifteen miles on each side of the road.

Grant—cool under pressure, as usual—sounded as if losing $1.5 million in supplies was just a minor inconvenience. Riding away from Holly Springs, Van Dorn was smiling, having extinguished his superiors' doubts about his ability to win a battle.

After destroying Grant's supplies at Holly Springs, Van Dorn and his troops rode toward Grand Junction, Tennessee. Despite having been in the center of the fighting, Holt and the Titus Grays found themselves engaged in fighting again on December 21 at Davis's Mill. When the fighting was over, twenty dead Texans lay on the field of battle. Burying their dead at Davis's Mill, the Texans rode hard across western Tennessee, destroying railroad tracks, burning bridges and wreaking havoc on Union supply lines. As the saying goes, "there is no rest for the weary," and throughout the rest of the month, Holt and the Texans were engaged in several other fights, losing more soldiers in the process.

Finally, Holt and his Texans were sent to Grenada, Mississippi, where they were given a much-needed furlough before being ordered to return to Tennessee. In February 1863, Van Dorn and his forces, including the Titus Grays, found themselves once again in a battle at Thompson's Station. On March 5, 1863, Union colonel John Coburn and his troops marched on the Confederate position, causing the Confederates to quickly abandon their posts. As the Confederates retreated, the Union troops entrenched themselves on the high ground overlooking Thompson's Station. Ordering his artillery to open fire to start the battle, Coburn quickly ordered an infantry charge on Thompson's Station. Charging downhill, the Union troops soon found themselves under intense fire from Confederate muskets. The battle seemed to be going as planned for the Union—until a bizarre confusion seemed to take over the Yankee troops.

For reasons unknown, Coburn's troops, without being ordered to do so, began to retreat en masse. Stunned, Coburn ordered them to halt, but his commands fell on deaf ears. Watching the Union retreat, Confederate

General Earl Van Dorn's decisive victory at Holly Springs, Mississippi, proved that he did have what it took to be effective as a commander. *Courtesy of Dickson College.*

general Nathan Bedford Forrest ordered his cavalry to ride due east and north to cut off their escape. Leading his troops toward the Union line, General Forrest and his cavalry were repulsed four times by the Union. During the fight, General Forrest had one of his favorite horses, Roderick, shot out from under him. Throughout the war, General Forrest would have thirty horses shot out from under him while engaged in battle. Years later, a Confederate veteran spoke of Thompson's Mill, saying the battle "continued…about five hours, so deadly and stubborn was the nature of the contest, that at times bayonets clashed and hand-to-hand fights were not uncommon." Eventually, exhausted and outnumbered, Coburn and his men surrendered. The Confederate victory was hard-fought, but it paid off as they captured 1,151 Union prisoners of war. Once again, Holt and his Texans had played a crucial role by attacking the center of the Union line.

Later in the year, Holt and the Texans, battle-worn and tired, were sent back to Mississippi to protect civilians and act as a police force against Union troops and renegades. Still led by Captain Perry Evans, the men of Company I scouted daily, which often lead to skirmishes with Union reconnaissance patrols. As winter set in, the men of the Ninth Texas Cavalry began to suffer from the cold as their uniforms wore thin from use. Howell Hinds, who had failed to raise a new artillery regiment, returned to Washington County and began to act as a partisan ranger with the Ninth Texas. Howell and Holt, together again, along with Captain Evans, began to delve into justice as they saw fit. The Ninth Texas, now left to their own devices, fought more like a guerrilla unit than a professional group of fighting men.

Chapter 7

MURDER, MAYHEM AND THE MILITIA

As 1863 faded into 1864, Holt Collier and the Titus Grays had spent the last sixteen months under little oversight from anyone other than Perry Evans. Acting as the judge, jury and executioner, the Titus Grays delivered a rough brand of frontier justice, even resorting to torturing some Northern sympathizers. Sam Worthington, describing the Ninth Texas Cavalry Company I, stated, "I verily believe that they would have braided the tail of a cyclone if commanded to do so by Captain Evans." As they drew closer together as a unit, Holt became even more accepted by these men, many of whom supported slavery. The irony of his part in this unit and the Civil War cannot go unnoticed.

One incident, related by Stevenson Archer, a military chaplain, gives us great insight into how Captain Perry Evans carried out his duties with a propensity for violence that shocked many Mississippians and angered others. On his way to perform a wedding ceremony, Chaplain Archer encountered Captain Evans on the road.

Ever suspicious, Evans asked Archer, "Where are you going, sir?"

Archer replied, "I am going to marry Miss Copeland to Lieutenant Johnson."

Captain Evans said, "It ain't no use, I have just had him shot and flung into the river."

Archer said, "Why, you are mistaken."

Stoned-faced, Captain Evans replied, "No, it is a fact."

Curious, Archer asked, "What did you do that for?"

"He stole Mr. Halsey's mules, and I had orders from General Forrest, who commands the cavalry in this section, to shoot all marauders, and simply executed my orders," Evans said finally, and he ride away.

Unsure if the information was correct, Chaplain Archer continued to Miss Copeland's house, where he found that the execution of Lieutenant Johnson and the disposal of his body was just as Captain Evans had stated. Whether the young lieutenant was guilty or innocent will never truly be known. This was just one of many examples of frontier justice dispensed by Perry Evans and his Texans. Their free rein would be short-lived, as the war was near its end.

On April 9, 1865, the two highest-ranking officers of the Civil War, the Confederates' Robert E. Lee and the Union's Ulysses S. Grant, met at Appomattox Court House, Virginia, to bring about an end to the war. Briefly acquainted with each other from their time in the Mexican War, the two men could not have been more different. Lee showed up to Wilmer McLean's in full military dress complete with sash and sword, while Grant showed up dressed in his field uniform, caked with mud. Regardless of their attire, Lee's surrender meant the end of a way of life for White Southerners and the beginning of a different life for the newly emancipated slaves. The house where Lee surrendered was owned by Wilmer McLean, whose house had been struck by a cannonball at the First Battle of Bull Run. Ironically, following the Battle of Bull Run, McLean moved to Appomattox Court House, Virginia, hoping to escape the war, only to have it come to an end in his parlor. Sources claim that McLean said, "The war began in my front yard and ended in my front parlor." No sooner had General Lee and Grant left the McLean house than looters descended on the home, attempting to grab any piece of history they could.

With the war at an end and his freedom granted, Holt had to decide whether to go back to the Plum Ridge Plantation and work for the Hinds family or strike out on his own. It was no surprise to anyone at Plum Ridge when they saw Holt, back straight, hat brim still turned upward, armed to the teeth, riding down the road toward the big house. Soon back in his routine, Holt found himself back by Howell's side. However, the Holt Collier who left Plum Ridge under the cover of darkness, a young, scared slave, had been replaced by a battle-tested veteran. The plantation had also changed: one of the gins had been burned by the Yankees, fences had been destroyed and other parts of the plantation were also damaged.

The Hinds family, which had been a dominant political and economic force in antebellum Mississippi, was now just one of many southern families

General Robert E. Lee was one of the most well-respected officers on either side during the war. He showed up to Appomattox Court House in full military dress. *Library of Congress.*

trying to put the pieces of their lives back together following the war. In the spring of 1866, Holt proved once again that he was Howell's most loyal and ardent supporter by saving his former master's life. The incident occurred when Holt entered Howell and his daughter Alice's room to help them get ready for the night. The train conductor, who would not stand for a Black man being in a White person's cabin, grabbed Holt and dragged him out like a "dog," Holt later stated. Flying into a rage, Howell shoved the conductor, who unsheathed a Bowie knife, threatening Howell. Shoving Howell aside, Holt drew his pistol and fired a round into the conductor's hip. Fortunately for Holt, Howell had many friends aboard the train. Howell was able to defuse the tense situation, which could have gone very badly for Holt.

After the war, Thomas Hinds was desperate to get his crops planted, his labor force was depleted and his back was up against a wall. Unfortunately, Thomas entered a deal that would turn Holt's life upside down. Desperate for laborers, Thomas turned to Greenville's chapter of the Freedman's Bureau for help. Headed by Captain James King, a former Union soldier, the

Freedman's Bureau provided former slaves with food, clothes and medical care. The bureau also helped former slaves find employment. However, like many carpetbaggers, Captain King hoped to use his position to personally profit from the desperation of southern planters.

With the 1866 planting season approaching quickly, Thomas Hinds entered a deal with Captain King to supply twenty-five Black laborers for the planting and harvesting of Plum Ridge's cotton crop. In exchange for the labor, Hinds would pay King fifty bales of cotton. Unfortunately for Thomas, his crop production was poor, and if he kept his end of the bargain, there would be very little, if any, cotton to sell at the market. Despite Thomas Hinds's urgency to renegotiate the contract, King would not budge. When Howell found out about Thomas's deal, he was furious.

Howell approached King on behalf of his son, and things turned ugly when the much older man was knocked to the ground by King, who pulled a knife. Holt's cousin, Rich Collier, stepped between the knife-wielding King and the elder Howell, disarming the situation. After the incident, for whatever reason, Captain King agreed to accept one bale of cotton per worker as payment, bringing the total to twenty-five instead of the agreed-on fifty bales. Three days before Christmas in 1866, Holt showed up at King's boarding house, inviting him to Plum Ridge to collect his payment. King saddled his horse, headed for Plum Ridge and was never seen alive again.

The next morning, December 23, King's riderless horse was found wandering through the streets of Greenville. Days later, the body of Captain James King, Civil War veteran and head of the Freedmen's Bureau, was found submerged beneath icy waters in a stand of canebrakes. King had been shot and his personal items taken from his body. With Holt having been the last person to call on King, the suspicion fell on the former slave and Confederate veteran. Arrested for murder, Holt was soon acquitted, but despite his exoneration, some people still believed he was guilty. With race relations between Blacks and Whites severely strained following the war in the South, Holt decided that as a Black man with an air of suspicion about the killing of a White man surrounding him, it would be best for his health to leave Mississippi. Saddling up his horse, he rode for Texas, where he would start a new life.

CHAPTER 8

LIFE AS A COWBOY

Today, Texas is America's second-most populated state, with 28.64 million people living within its borders; however, in 1867, there were just 604,215 Texans occupying the state's 268,597 square miles. Many of its residents in 1867 were former slaves, forced to make their living as sharecroppers. Renting land from White owners under rigorous conditions, they often found themselves under a new form of oppression. A third of the sharecroppers in the South were Black following the war, while two thirds were poor Whites. Despite sharecroppers being on the bottom rung of the socioeconomic and social ladder, White sharecroppers were considered a step above former slaves due to their race.

Having rarely worked in the fields as a child, Holt Collier had no intention of starting when he arrived in Texas. As a man who could rope, ride and shoot, he hoped to make his living as a cowboy. Holt was not alone, as 25 percent of cowboys in the West during the late 1800s were African American. Cowboying was a profession where men were judged more by their abilities than their race. During the famous Lincoln County War, Pete Staples, a former Texas slave, achieved notoriety as a Black cowboy who rode in some of the first cattle drives from Texas to Kansas. Those early cattle drives, with the help of the railroad, allowed people from the East and West Coasts access to fresh beef.

As did all cowboys, Holt had to prove his worth in the saddle before being hired by Louis Sullivan Ross, a large ranch owner. Riding into Ross's ranch, Holt caught the eye of other cowboys, who sized up the young Black

Bill Pickett became famous for his skills as an African American cowboy. He was credited for inventing the method of bulldogging cattle. *Courtesy of the Norman Silent Movie Studios.*

man from Mississippi. Ross soon put Holt's skills to the test, asking him to ride a mustang that had not been broken. Never one to back down from a challenge, Holt climbed onto the mustang's back and held on for dear life. As the mustang tried to rid itself of its rider, Holt stayed in the saddle, bending the young mustang to his will. In an account about breaking the mustang, Holt said, "After a while I turned 'im 'roun' and rid back to camp, jes' as nice an' easy as ef I was a lady goin' to church." After his success with the mustang, Ross and the other cowboys decided that Holt had earned his spurs.

On the open plains of Texas, Holt relished the ability to ride his horse as far as his eye could see. Texas's nights were also special, as the horizon was lit with what seemed like every star in the galaxy. Texas also teemed with wild game: whitetail deer, bobcats, antelope, mountain lions, coyotes, wolves and more were abundant throughout the state. As a man who loved hunting, Holt was excited to hang so many species that didn't live in Mississippi. Traveling to Texas also gave him a chance to visit with his old commander and friend Perry Evans. Evans and Holt, who shared a mutual respect, relished being reunited.

Louis Sullivan Ross, Holt's boss, a former Confederate general, had also fought at the Battle of Corinth. Much like Holt, Ross's life had been one of great adventure even before leaving Texas to join the Confederacy. Before the war, Ross joined the Texas Rangers, fighting battles against several Native American tribes. While with the Rangers, he was involved in rescuing Cynthia Ann Parker, the most famous Native American captive in American history. Taken by the Comanches at age nine, Cynthia spent twenty-four years among the Native American tribe. Eventually, she married a Comanche warrior named Peta Nocona, and they had several children together. Taken by Ross and the other Texas Rangers, she failed to adjust to life among Whites and died in 1871. Following the Civil War, Ross was elected to the office of governor of Texas, served as the president of Texas A&M University and increased his ranch to around one thousand acres. Holt would always remember Ross as the man who took a chance on a former slave who had fled Mississippi.

With practice, Holt became a first-class cow hand who could rope, ride and break horses with the best of Ross's men. His success as a cowboy was only diminished by his longing to return to Plum Ridge and the Hinds family. Back in Mississippi, the Hinds family had not fared as well as Holt. With the South's postwar economy in shambles, Howell Hinds's debts began to mount, and before long, he was forced to sell his beloved Home Hill Plantation. With his family in tow, Howell moved north to Plum Ridge. To the Hinds women, accustomed to a world of entertaining, lavish dresses and a more civilized area, Plum Ridge still seemed a rugged wilderness.

Despite Howell's fall from his social and economic pedestal, Thomas's life proved to be even more scandalous when, in 1867, he began to cohabitate with Augusta Collier. No one is sure what happened to Thomas's legal wife, Victoria Sullivan, and with no record of her ever giving birth, no record of a divorce and no death certificate, she seems to have vanished without a trace. Most likely, it was Thomas's relationship with Augusta that led to him being formally charged with fornication. The charges against him were eventually dropped, but the stigma of immorality hung over him for the rest of his life. Augusta, who had been gifted to Thomas by his father in July 1861, was Holt's younger sister. It seems that the lovers were very dedicated to one another, remaining together for the rest of Thomas's life. Their relationship, which neither of them tried to conceal, would have garnered a lot of negative attention during a time when interracial

Sharecropping and the cotton industry were part of Mississippi's lifeblood following the war. However, they could not save Howell Hind's Plum Ridge Plantation. *Library of Congress.*

relationships were relatively unheard of. The couple went on to have six children together.

Still fearful of returning to Mississippi, Holt could not keep himself away when he heard that his old master, Howell Hinds, had been murdered. The *Memphis Avalanche*, a daily newspaper, reported Howell's murder on May 17. According to an eyewitness, Colonel Hinds was attempting to keep Major E.P. Byrnes and Dr. T.G. Polk from coming to blows when Dr. O.M. Blanton crept up behind Colonel Hinds armed with a large Bowie knife. Before bystanders could act, Blanton stabbed Hinds three times, mortally wounding him. After attacking Hinds, Blanton stabbed Major Byrne and Captain B.G. Sims and ran into the woods. Fearing for his life, Blanton fled to Europe, entering a self-imposed exile. After he felt like the coast was clear, he returned to the States to live with his mother in New Jersey. Many years later, Blanton claimed that he killed Colonel Hinds and stabbed Major Byrnes in self-defense.

When news reached Texas, Holt was furious that his former master and friend had been murdered. Throwing caution to the wind, Collier was determined to find the man who killed Colonel Hinds and exact revenge on him. Riding back into the Mississippi Delta, where he was still under suspicion for the murder of Captain James King, Holt soon found Union troops harassing him at every turn. One day, he was heckled by a group of Union soldiers for his role as a Confederate soldier. Pulling his pistol, Holt fired a shot toward his abusers. While none of the soldiers were harmed, Holt found himself in hot water. Not sure what to do, Holt turned to Thomas Hinds for help. Approaching the unit's officer, Thomas explained the situation, apologized and asked for the officer to speak to his men on Holt's behalf. The officer agreed and set his men straight, and Collier had no further trouble from them.

With Blanton long gone and Holt's devotion to the Hinds family still running deep, he returned home to Plum Ridge Plantation. His mother and father, Daphne and Harrison, were well advanced in years, but their relationship with Thomas Hinds was still strong—stronger, even, now that Hinds was their unofficial son-in-law. The death of Howell Hinds and the loss of their social and political standing, hung heavily over the Hinds family. With his usual gusto, Holt began to work the fields, but no matter how much he and the Hindses scratched in the fertile Mississippi soil, they were unable to save the plantation. The loss of Plum Ridge marked the end of an era for the Hinds and Collier families.

CHAPTER 9

FROM COWBOY TO PROFESSIONAL HUNTER

One of the main stipulations of the Reconstruction Act of 1867 required former Confederate states to include a universal suffrage clause in their new constitutions. Almost immediately, Mississippi was torn apart by political turmoil. Under federal supervision, the political landscape of Alabama, Mississippi and South Carolina, whose Black residents outnumbered White citizens, changed almost overnight. With Mississippi divided into Republican and Democratic factions, many carpetbaggers tried to exert political influence to control the economy in their favor. Holt was not immune to this turmoil, as he was approached by some political factions to use his influence to drum up votes. They also wanted Holt to strongarm people for votes. The offers were backed with large sums of money, but Holt turned them all down.

As America's economy began to wane, the integration of former slaves into southern society took a back seat to economic survival. In 1877, the federal government pulled up roots from the South, and Reconstruction came to an end. Most of the progress that the Reconstruction governments had achieved ended as Jim Crow laws were established, separating Blacks from Whites. With federal voting supervision no longer an option, southern states designed ways to keep Blacks from voting, implementing poll taxes and literacy exams. To circumvent the rules for poor Whites, the grandfather clause was established, which allowed any White man whose father or grandfather actively voted before 1867 to vote regardless of the restrictions. With regulations such as those, the cards would be stacked against African

General Nathan Bedford Forrest, known as the "Wizard of the Saddle," was one of the founding members of the Ku Klux Klan in Pulaski, Tennessee. *Courtesy of Wikimedia Commons.*

Americans, such as Holt Collier, in the realms of education and voting for the next one hundred years.

African Americans also had to face the wrath of a new organization that was founded during the dark hours of Christmas Eve 1865. Riding through the cold night, former members of the Confederacy met in Pulaski, Tennessee, to form a social club that would evolve into a paramilitary organization that would work toward reversing the progress made by African Americans during Reconstruction. Former Confederate general Nathan Bedford Forest, a man who, during the Civil War, tried to convince Holt Collier to scout and fight with his cavalry, became the first grand wizard of the KKK. Wearing white sheets, the KKK spread its brand of terror throughout African American communities with lynchings, cross burnings and beatings. According to the *Washington Post*, between 1877 and 1950, four thousand lynchings of men, women and even children, took place throughout the United States; Mississippi led the nation with 581 lynchings during that period.

Other changes came for Mississippi and Holt as large-scale plantation farming became no longer feasible due to the lack of slave labor and people in Mississippi began to look for other avenues in which to make money. By the late 1800s, Mississippi was home to an estimated 24.975 million feet of yellow pine. A versatile wood, yellow pine was used to build houses, furniture and cabinetry, placing it in high demand. With Americans building more and more homes to replace those destroyed in the Civil War, Mississippi saw a huge increase in the number of new sawmills. Many men who had farmed before the war took up axes and crosscut saws, heading to Mississippi's vast wilderness to make their living in a new economic era. Holt Collier, trying to escape the chains of sharecropping, decided to make a living from what he knew best: hunting.

Due to the lumber boom, lumber companies were struggling to feed their growing workforces. Where some people see problems, others see solutions, and Holt saw his way out of sharecropping in the teeming game of the Mississippi Delta. Using his superior hunting skills, he sold bear and deer carcasses to lumber companies to help feed their employees. A full-sized black bear carcass brought around sixty dollars. A whitetail deer would earn Holt thirty cents per pound when field dressed. People often say, "Do what you love, and you will never work a day in your life"—well, Holt was doing what he loved and making great money in the process. Even though he needed money to survive, he was never enamored of it. He made it plain how he felt about money when he said, "Money don't buy nothing in the canebrake, no how. And a man's dog does not care whether he is rich or poor."

As the Mississippi became more industrialized, the transportation of goods became a real concern, which brought about the rise of railroad construction. Between 1865 and 1880, 120 miles of new railroad tracks were laid in Mississippi, and this number steadily increased for the next three decades. With large workforces laying track, Holt began to provide the railroad companies with meat. Many seasons, Holt harvested 125 bears or more, making a huge profit for any man, Black or White, during the late 1800s. However, as Holt and others like him continued to kill bears for food and sport, Mississippi's black bear population began to dwindle.

Before the influx of the Spanish and the Anglo-Saxons into what is now Mississippi, the black bear was killed by Native Americans for food and clothing. Archaeological findings have shown that Native Americans also used black bears in religious ceremonies and for trade to the Europeans in the 1500s. As settlements started to grow in Mississippi, people began to see black bears as a nuisance to their crops and livestock. Settlers began to kill bears whenever they encountered them. In Mississippi's antebellum days, the bear population was so high that plantation owners would often post a

An unidentified hunter carrying the black bear he bagged over his shoulder. *Library of Congress. Photograph by Earle D. Akin Co.*

slave at night outside their livestock pens to raise an alarm at the sight of a bear. As time passed, men began to hunt black bears for sport, adding to their decline in the state.

Today, Mississippi has a very small bear population, with two subspecies of black bears. The American black bear lives mainly in the northern half of Mississippi, and the Louisiana black bear occupies the southern half of the state. The black bear is the smallest of all breeds of bears in the United States, with the male of the species weighing between 150 and 350 pounds, while the females weigh between 120 and 250 pounds. Today, Mississippi's black bears are found in three areas of Mississippi: the Mississippi River Delta, the Gulf Coast and the Loess Bluffs of Southwest Mississippi. Black bears, who are labeled as carnivores, survive mostly on plant-based material. With plant-based material abundant throughout the state, black bears rarely go hungry. Bears supplement their diet with protein from insects and carrion, which is the decaying flesh of dead animals.

As more hunters began to flood the state, Mississippi's black bear population began to plummet, and the newly formed Mississippi Game and Fish Commission shut down black bear hunting in 1932. With repopulation in mind, the Mississippi Game and Fish Commission released three pairs of black bears in 1934 to prevent their extinction from the state. According to the Mississippi Department of Wildlife, Fisheries & Parks (MDWFP), there are over one hundred black bears in the state. The MDWFP is working hard to trap and collar many of the black bears to learn more about their habits and travel patterns. With habitats being restored, especially in the Mississippi Delta, experts are very hopeful that the black bear population will soon be on the rise.

Chapter 10

RAGS TO RICHES

Back in his element, Holt relished crashing through the Mississippi canebrakes chasing his dogs in pursuit of black bears. As his reputation as a hunter grew, so did his pack of hunting dogs. Holt had been introduced to hunting dogs early in life as he was ordered, along with his brother, to help take care of the large pack of dogs Master Howell Hinds kept on his plantation. Most of Holt's dogs, like those of other bear hunters of the time, were a hodgepodge of breeds and sizes, but they all had one thing in common: they were tough. Holt said of his dogs, "My dogs would fight a bear three or four days an' nights until they 'most starved to death, waitin' for me to come. I often found 'em the third or fourth day treein' or fightin'. Me and them both has lived off o' raw meat, an' not cared whether 'twere cooked or not." His statement gives us a glimpse of the measure of pride he took in raising, training and running his dogs.

Collier's skills became so profitable as a meat hunter that he was known to carry as much as $2,000 with him. Adjusting for inflation, that would be around $45,000 today. Most people would have been fearful of carrying that much money, but Holt was not like most people. Heavily armed and not opposed to killing, he would have been a dangerous man to rob. The Civil War, as it did for many men, hardened Holt, causing him to often shoot first and ask questions later. Following the war, Mississippi needed men of action, as lawlessness was not unusual, especially in the Delta. Holt would eventually help fill the need for good, sound men who were willing to protect others.

Holt Collier mounted and ready for the hunt. He is dressed in the same style as he was during his time with the Ninth Texas Cavalry. Note the large pack of dogs awaiting orders from Holt. *Courtesy of Wikimedia Commons.*

Despite being a successful man, who could have easily bought a house, Holt preferred to live in tents rather than establish roots in one place. Storing his belongings at his brother Marshall's home and a local stable, he chose to camp in the swamps where he hunted. In a tent or under the stars, he was lulled to sleep by the chirping of crickets and the croaking of bullfrogs. He survived on a diet of wild game, supplemented by goods he purchased at the dry goods store in Greenville and food he gathered from the swamp. Cooking over a campfire and bathing in the swamp or nearby creeks, he relished living outdoors. Throughout the state, others lived similar lifestyles, making their money chasing black bears and other wild game.

By 1890, Robert Eager Bobo, born in 1847 in Panola County, Mississippi, had also gained a reputation as a world-class bear hunter. Bobo's eighty dogs made up one of the largest, if not the largest, pack of hunting dogs in the state. Unlike many bear hunters, Bobo very rarely used a gun while hunting; instead he used a Dahlgren navy Bowie-style Civil War bayonet to kill bears when his dogs had them cornered. Bobo claimed to have killed as many as 304 bears, 21 deer, 17 panthers and 47 wildcats from September

1873 to September 1874. With a reputation as a first-class bear hunter, he guided many people on bear hunts throughout the Mississippi Delta. According to Kit Dalton, Bobo even hosted a bear hunt for the infamous outlaw Jesse James. Having spent his life fearlessly riding his horse full speed through canebrakes and cypress knees, living outdoors and killing bears armed only with a knife, Bobo eventually died in bed in Chicago, Illinois, of complications from an emergency medical procedure.

Another famous bear hunter, born after Holt Collier, was Benjamin Vernon Lilly. Lilly was born on a cold New Year's Eve in 1856 in Wilcox County, Alabama. When he was a young boy, his family relocated to Kemper County, Mississippi, where he grew to love the outdoors. Moving from Mississippi to Tennessee and then Louisiana, Lilly eventually found his calling in life as a bear hunter. Exceptionally strong, Lilly often left his guns at home, arming himself only with a knife while hunting. Lilly passed away in 1936 just two weeks shy of his eightieth birthday.

Bear hunters, whether they were Holt Collier or one of the others who obtained fame, possessed a certain set of skills and qualities. One of their greatest shared qualities was their thirst for adventure and danger. Rushing into the canebrakes face-to-face with an angry bear took real grit, determination and bravery. As professional guides, they also had to look out for the well-being of their clients, many of whom were inexperienced in

Holt Collier surrounded by a group of unidentified hunters who employed his services as a guide. *Courtesy of the Heritage Post.*

Teddy Roosevelt was known for his large, toothy grin. *Library of Congress.*

such intense situations. With dogs barking, men shouting and a bear roaring, guides required laser-like focus to ensure that no one got injured and they were able to bag their prey.

When Holt began his business as a meat hunter, there was not much, if anything, he didn't know about black bear hunting. When not running his dogs, he employed the spot and stalk method, which requires a great deal of skill. With a keen sense of smell, black bears can oftentimes smell hunters long before they see them. A good hunter, like Holt, stays downwind of a bear, making sure that the bear never catches his scent. With triangular ears and stereophonic hearing, bears can hear the slightest movements. A good hunter can slip through the woods like a ghost, avoiding stepping on limbs and dry leaves and other noisy pitfalls. If they fail to be diligent in any one of these duties, the bear will bolt, leaving the hunter empty-handed. A seasoned tracker can even determine the sex of a bear from the depth of its tracks.

Heat and humidity are often a bear hunter's worst enemy. When harvesting a bear in warm weather, time is of the essence, or else the meat will spoil. Butchering a bear takes skill and requires a steady hand because if the knife punctures the bear's stomach or intestines, the meat can become contaminated. Because deer are harvested in cooler weather, they can be field dressed improperly without serious consequences. Bear hunters, on the other hand, must field dress exactly right if they hope to maintain the integrity of the meat. Skinning a bear, especially if the hunter wants to preserve the pelt for a trophy, is a tedious and worrisome process. Throughout his years as a guide, Holt Collier sent many of his clients home with a pelt that would be mounted in either a full-body mount or a head mount or turned into a bearskin rug.

As bear hunting became more of a sport than a necessity, people flooded into Mississippi for the thrill of the hunt. Men with deep pockets and a thirst for adventure sought out Holt to take them on the hunt of a lifetime. Holt was happy to oblige them if they paid his fee and abided by his rules. As a professional guide and hunter, Holt's reputation began to be known throughout the United States and would eventually grab the attention of one of the greatest hunters in history, Teddy Roosevelt.

CHAPTER 11

GAMBLING AND RAMBLING

As different as Holt Collier and Howell Hinds were, they had one thing in common: they both loved to gamble. As much as he abhorred the vice of alcohol, Holt Collier could not shake his gambling addiction. He loved any game of chance, from cards to dice, but most of all, he loved to gamble on horses. Horses had always been a big part of his life; from his days at the Home Hill Plantation and Plum Ridge to his time as a cavalry soldier and bear hunter, they were special to him. As a rider and observer of horses, Holt was a fine judge of horseflesh and used his knowledge to gamble on the mounts he deemed the fastest.

When hunting season closed, Holt would saddle up his favorite horse and travel wherever there was a horse race or poker game. He found no lack of either as he ranged as far west as Texas and as far south as Louisiana. When asked about his gambling, Collier said,

> *In the spring I'd go away an foller the races same as I used to—St. Louis an' Saratoga an' New Orleans, an' way out in Texas takin in the fairs. Then in the fall I'd come home, git my dogs together and hit the cane-brake again—I jes nacherly loved a hoss and loved to hunt bears. Didn't do much 'cept hunt.*

The fairs Holt came to love were a strange mixture of family entertainment, rides, food and gambling. Many times, when he returned to Mississippi

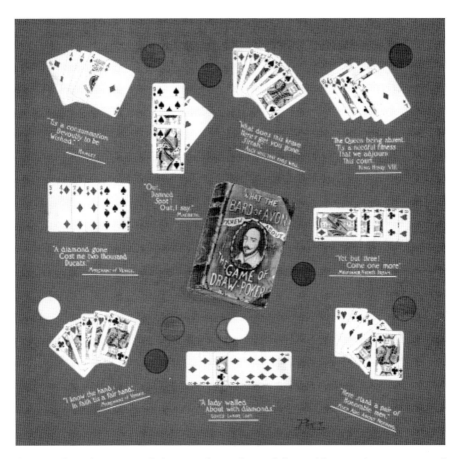

Outside of hunting, games of chance such as poker and dice and horse racing were some of Holt Collier's favorite hobbies. *Courtesy of Fine Art America.*

from his trips abroad, the large wad of cash he carried with him would be depleted. When he returned home, he would hit the woods and canebrakes, attempting to regain some of his lost income. On several occasions, Thomas Hinds tried to talk Holt out of going on his gambling trips, but to no avail. Holt said, "Ev'ry time I put my hand in there [his pocket] an' felt a dollar I cotch the travel itch, until I jes' couldn't keep off'n the train."

By 1880, Holt had a reason to stay closer to home: he had gotten married to a woman named Rose. This was most likely a common law marriage, as there are no marriage records in existence listing Holt Collier and Rose as a couple. In 1880 Mississippi, a common law marriage could be established when a man and woman shared property or a dwelling or considered themselves married. The State of Mississippi did away with common law marriage in 1956 and no longer recognizes a couple's right to inherit each other's possessions unless specified in one of their wills.

With marriage comes children, and Rose eventually gave birth to two daughters, Effy and Maggie, and one son, Coley. With extra mouths to feed and a gambling habit, Holt worked as a part-time deputy for Major George Helm, the sheriff in nearby Stoneville, Mississippi. Today's Stoneville is unincorporated, with a population of forty-four residents. In the late 1800s, the town was home to a jail where some of the county's worst offenders were often held before being tried and sent off to state prison. Occasionally, when an especially hated criminal was being held, the residents of Stoneville would march on the jail to impose vigilante justice. When Helm believed this might happen, he would hire Holt, place a double-barreled shotgun in his hand and seat him in front of the jail. Standing guard, Holt was never challenged by a mob. The fact that Holt, an African American, was allowed so much responsibility in postwar Mississippi was unusual and lends further insight into how highly respected he was in the Delta.

As the years passed, Holt's exploits in law enforcement became more varied and dangerous. Of course, a man not afraid to go after a cornered bear with only a knife would not be backed down by other men. Also, his duties as a deputy, even when he was forced to take a life, were mild compared to the carnage he saw and participated in during the war. Although he'd killed before, there is no evidence that Holt took pleasure in killing another human—but when it came to defending himself, he would not hesitate to shoot.

It was May 1881, a sweltering and humid month for Mississippi, when violence erupted between the Lott brothers and Deputy Travis Elmore Sage. In the late 1800s, the line between lawmen and outlaws was often blurred. For many years following the Civil War, Louisiana was a hotbed for political arguments, often leading to violence, which happened on May 24 in West Carroll Parish, Louisiana. Travis Sage, who had been hired by Bill "Wildcat" Bradley as a deputy for the parish, spent most of his time drinking and gambling at a local saloon. On the evening of the twenty-fourth, he was stationed outside the saloon when up rode Richard Lott. Unfortunately, Sage began to belittle Richard and his family. Without warning, Sage blasted Richard from the saddle, killing him instantly.

Nearby, Jesse Lott, a small business owner and Richard's brother, heard the shots and rushed to his brother's lifeless body. Anger clouding his judgment, Jesse took Richard's pistol in hand, aimed at Sage, who was scrambling for his mount, and pulled the trigger three times. Unfortunately for Jesse, the gun misfired all three times. Whirling, Sage fired, wounding Jesse mortally. Not sure if he would be accused or tried for murder, Sage spurred his horse onward, disappearing into the darkness. Fleeing, Sage implied his guilt in the death of the Lott brothers. As Richard and Jesse were men of prominence in the parish, their deaths would not go unanswered.

Early in July, Holt was scouting for bears in the Mississippi swamp when he ran into a constable who told him about the murder of the Lott brothers. The constable mentioned that a man fitting Sage's description had been spotted nearby. The constable, familiar with Holt's reputation as a tough man, asked him to investigate the man's identity before he crossed the Bogue Phalia River. Holt's investigation proved that the man they suspected to be Sage was the killer of the Lott brothers. During his investigation, Holt found out that Sage was living under an assumed name. "Stacks," as Sage was known, was hoping to cross the river and disappear into the Mississippi swamps.

Catching up with Sage at Washburn's Ferry, Holt devised a plan to capture him without firing a shot. Mentioning that he admired Sage's Winchester rifle, Holt asked if he could hold it. Recognizing the famous hunter, Sage obliged and handed over his weapon. It was only then, after Sage had been disarmed, that Holt informed him about the warrant for his arrest. Whether because of his refusal to be arrested by a Black lawman or fear of being hanged, history can never be fully sure, but Sage decided that he was not going down without a fight. Sage, who was mounted, spurred his horse forward, pinning Collier against a rail. Sage called for one of his friends to pass him their rifle so he could dispose of Holt. As he brought the gun into shooting position, Sage's horse spooked, allowing Holt a moment to draw his pistol and take aim. Firing quickly, Holt blasted the outlaw from his saddle. Whether by luck or skill, Holt walked away without a scratch.

Holt, aware that killing a White man put him in precarious situation, turned himself over to the authorities. Luckily for Holt, Sage had such a seedy reputation that the question of anything but self-defense never came into play. With the killing of Sage, Holt's reputation as a man not to be trifled with was firmly established throughout Greenville and the surrounding areas. A violent, ill-tempered man who stayed drunk much of the time, Sage had few mourners as he was buried in Greenville, Mississippi.

CHAPTER 12.

FROM MEAT HUNTER TO PROFESSIONAL GUIDE

At the close of the 1800s, railroads and massive farming had destroyed a huge amount of black bear habitat. With the destruction of their habitat and overhunting, Mississippi's black bear population was in serious decline by 1890. For a man who made much of his money through meat hunting, Holt had to rethink the way he made a living. With the black bear population still high, he decided that he could make a living as a hunting guide. Investing in himself and his skill set, Holt created a first-class guide service. His service was all-inclusive, providing wagons, camping gear, dogs and even a camp cook. His investment quickly paid off as clients began to book his services.

Not only did Holt change professions in the late 1800s, but he also changed wives. No one is sure what happened to Rose Collier, but in December 1890, Holt obtained a license to marry Maggie Phillips. Strangely, there are also no records that exist lending insight into what happened to Holt and Rose's children. Oddly enough, very little is also known about Maggie Phillips. Holt's lack of dedication to monogamy was unusual in the Collier family, as his parents, Daphne and Harrison, stayed married until Harrison's death. Thomas Hinds and Holt's sister, Augusta, also stayed together for the duration of their lives, siring the only known descendants of General Thomas Hinds.

As his reputation as a hunting guide grew, men with money and a sense of adventure poured into the Mississippi Delta for the hunt of a lifetime. With the bear population reduced in Washington County, Holt moved

A charcoal drawing of Holt from 1885. No one, not even Holt, would have guessed that his name would be forever tied to Teddy Roosevelt. *Sketch by William Von Dresser.*

his operations south to the swampy counties of Issaquena and Sharkey. Located along the Mississippi-Arkansas border, Issaquena County was named for a Native American phrase that translates to "deer river." With the state's ninth-most-valuable farmland during Mississippi's antebellum years, Issaquena had a large slave workforce. By 1900, Issaquena's average farm size was only fifty-five acres, which left much of the county's acreage unused, allowing it to become a haven for wildlife, including black bears. Sharkey County was formed from parts of Washington, Issaquena and Warren Counties and was dominated by sharecropping following the Civil War. It would become a hotbed for black bear hunting. Today, both Issaquena and Sharkey Counties have relatively small populations made up mostly of African Americans.

Before the integration of professional sports by such men as Jack Johnson, heavyweight boxing champion; Jackie Robinson, the first Black man to play in the Major Leagues; and others who paved the way for African Americans in the world of sports, the sport of hunting brought Whites and Blacks together in the pursuit of wild game. Holt's skills and reputation provided him the opportunity to rub elbows with powerful and wealthy White men. Holt's standing among these men was built on his reputation for bravery in the face of adversity. One of his most well-known feats of bravery happened when a bear cornered one of his favorite dogs in a hollow tree. Without hesitation, Collier crawled inside the tree, armed with only a knife, to save his dog from what he feared was imminent death. Coming face-to-face with the angry bear, Holt acted quickly, stabbing the bear to death as it tried to crawl past him. Amazingly, Holt suffered only minor scratches.

Clive and Harley Metcalfe were two of the White men who frequently sought out Holt's company and advice when it came to hunting. Like many of the White men Holt had contact with, the Metcalfe brothers were wealthy and powerful. The two brothers had their hands in many prosperous ventures throughout the Delta, holding positions with the Commercial National Bank of Greenville, the Greenville Compress Company, the Hotel Greenville and the Delta Compress Company. However, as busy as they were, they always made time to go hunting, and they always included Holt Collier in their adventures. Of course, as much as they enjoyed Holt's company, his friendship came with benefits. Being friends with Holt gave them access to one of the greatest packs of hunting dogs in the entire Delta, if not the state of Mississippi.

Very organized, the Metcalfe brothers kept a careful ledger of their hunting adventures. With Holt's name appearing frequently throughout the ledger, their friendship cannot be denied. Their journal also gives testimony to the fact that the black bear population was in rapid decline around Greenville, as they wrote on October 1, 1893, "Harley came and we went out hunting did not start a single thing. The bear have all but disappeared from this part of the country." Several other entries lamented their poor luck in hunting, stating that they had found no game, especially bears. With such powerful and influential friends, Holt's guide service blossomed into a profitable living.

On Sunday, January 10, 1897, the *Sun*, a New York newspaper, published an account of a bear hunt led by Holt in the Mississippi Delta. The author stated that Holt, at the time, was between fifty and sixty years old. The newspaper article dubbed Holt the "King of the Mississippi Bear Hunters." The article gives the reader a firsthand account of what it was like to chase bears through the Mississippi canebrakes and hear the baying of the dogs. Camped in a small muslin tent, Holt started the hunt early in the morning, releasing Sally and Rover, two of his eighteen hunting dogs. After about half an hour, with sixteen dogs at heel, Holt heard a dog bay and exclaimed, "Dat's Rover! Rover's got him. Listen!" As the group of hunters stopped, they listened intently before hearing Rover's long bay in the distance. After a few minutes, Sally joined in, and the hunt was on. With the two main dogs in the lead, Holt signaled for the whole pack to be released.

Holt rode his horse at a breakneck speed, and the other hunters had difficulty keeping up with him through the thick swamps. Their ride ended at a massive growth of canebrakes; dismounting, the men ran alongside it. Finally, Holt shouted, "He am treed!" Obeying his orders, the hunting party charged into the canebrakes, where they soon found the bear. As the hunting party approached a cypress tree, Holt said, "Doan yo' see him? Doan yo' see dat bah?" Sure enough, there, peering out from the branches of the cypress, was the face of a decent-sized black bear. The bear dropped from the tree, and chaos ensued as the pack fought the angry beast. The author of the article fired one shot, which passed through the bear, and another shot that struck the bear in its hips. Still fighting, the beast ran one hundred feet before it fell dead. The bear, which weighed around two hundred pounds field dressed, had taken the hunters twelve miles from camp through rough forest terrain and thick canebrakes. It was well after dark when the hunters returned to their meager camp with their trophy in tow.

The next morning, the hunters were at it again, this time joined by a man named Planter Bradley. With eight dogs in tow, Bradley set his dogs loose with Holt's, and they were quickly on the trail of a bear who crashed through the canebrakes growling and fighting. Standing on its hind legs, the bear was quickly overcome by the pack of frenzied dogs. Fighting for its life, the bear snapped its powerful jaws, killing one of Holt's hounds. Swinging its deadly paws, the bear killed two more dogs, thinning the pack. Seizing an opening, the author squeezed off three shots in rapid succession. Crashing to the ground, the bear breathed his last. The bear was much bigger than the one the day before, requiring five men working ropes to haul the beast on the back of a horse. Field-dressed, the bear weighed 375 pounds, which would have made it around 500 pounds before it was dressed. There were countless other hunts like this one, but not until November 1902 would Holt become a local legend.

CHAPTER 13

PREPARING FOR THE PRESIDENT

It was on October 27, 1858, that our twenty-sixth president, Theodore Roosevelt—or Teddy, as many people called him—came into the world. A screaming, red-faced baby boy, born into a world of privilege, would become one of the most beloved figures in American history. Teddy was stricken with debilitating childhood asthma, and his father, Theodore Roosevelt Sr., believed that his son needed to exercise vigorously. Beginning a regimen of weightlifting, boxing, running and swimming, Teddy was able to control his asthma, becoming a vigorous adult who sought adventure at every turn.

In 1880, Teddy met and married wealthy socialite Alice Hathaway. Unfortunately, his marriage was a short one, as Alice died from Bright's disease on Valentine's Day 1884 after giving birth to their first daughter, Alice Lee Roosevelt. Eleven hours before Alice passed away, Teddy's mother had died from typhoid fever. Sadly, the two most important women in his life were buried in a double ceremony. Devastated by grief, Teddy left his new daughter with his sister Anna, known as "Bamie," and headed to North Dakota. Working on his ranch, herding cattle and hunting, Teddy eventually came out from under his grief. Despite not seeing his daughter during those two years he spent in the Dakotas, he wrote to his sister frequently inquiring about and professing his love for his little Alice, whom he dubbed Baby Lee. Eventually, he returned to civilization and traveled to London, where he met and married Edith Carow in 1886. Edith would eventually become the First Lady of the United States, mother to Teddy's five children and stepmother to Alice Lee.

Colonel Teddy Roosevelt is at the center of the Rough Riders. His role in the Spanish-American War would be his springboard to national politics. *Library of Congress. Photograph by William Dinwiddie.*

Two years after Teddy married Edith, the United States declared war on Spain, and he sprang into action, resigning his position as assistant secretary of the navy to organize a cavalry unit named the Rough Riders. Shipped to Cuba, Roosevelt and the Rough Riders seized a piece of history as they captured Kettle Hill and then participated in the famous charge of San Juan Hill. His heroism and bravery in the war, which he recalled in several personal accounts, made Roosevelt a household name. People thought Teddy's sense of adventure would have been quenched by battle, but the Spanish-American War only fanned the flames of his adventurous spirit. Returning home from Cuba, Roosevelt entered politics and was elected governor of New York in 1898.

With his connections and political acumen, he soon found himself being considered for the vice presidency of the United States. Running as a

Twenty-fifth president of the United States William McKinley was shot down by Leon Czolgosz. When McKinley passed away, Teddy Roosevelt became the youngest president in American history. *Library of Congress. Photograph by Charles Parker.*

Republican, Teddy was elected as vice president under William McKinley in the election of 1900. Unbeknownst to Teddy, McKinley and the United States, McKinley had very little time to live. On September 14, 1901, President McKinley was in Buffalo, New York, making an appearance at the Pan-American Exposition when Leon Czolgosz, an anarchist, shot the president with a .32-caliber revolver concealed beneath a handkerchief. Today, the gun that was used to shoot President McKinley is on display at the Buffalo History Museum.

Teddy was in Vermont, prepared to give a speech to the Vermont Fish and Game League, when he was told that the president had been shot. Rushing to the train station, he traveled to Buffalo where he found the doctors were optimistic about McKinley's condition after operating on the wounded president. Assured by doctors that McKinley would make a recovery, Teddy left for the Adirondack Mountains to vacation with his family. Unfortunately, the doctors were wrong, and William McKinley passed away on September 14, 1901, eight days after being shot. Back in Buffalo, Teddy was sworn in at the Wilcox house as the twenty-sixth president of the United States. At forty-two, he became the youngest president in American history.

With his usual aplomb, he grabbed the bull by the horns and became a champion for the common people. He believed it was his responsibility to protect average Americans from the large industrialists or robber barons that were preying on them. Teddy believed in protecting the American public by any means necessary if his actions were not unconstitutional. Teddy once wrote, "I did not usurp power, but I did greatly broaden the use of executive power." As a man of the people, he quickly endeared himself to the American public, but even the pressures of public office could not quench his desire for hunting and the outdoors. It was his desire for the hunt that led him to cross paths with Holt Collier in 1902.

Mississippi, known for its abundance of game, had been on the president's mind for quite some time before he was invited on a hunt by Mississippi's Governor Andrew Longino. Longino, a moderate Democrat, was Mississippi's first governor since the Civil War and was not a veteran of the War Between the States. Teddy held nothing against the governor, but he did voice some concern over the large number of people that were invited to the hunt. In a letter to John Parker, Teddy wrote,

> *I am sure you will not misunderstand me when I say that I trust every effort will be made to have me get the chance to kill a bear…..Now when I hunt I go purely and simply to get game and to enjoy the wilderness while doing so, and the only hesitancy I had about going on this trip was lest we might have too many men, and it might result in my not getting a bear.*

Believing too many people would tag along, Teddy first turned down the governor's invitation, much to the excitement of many people in Mississippi. In November 1902, a newspaper in northeast Mississippi wrote,

> *President Roosevelt has the declared his intention not to visit Mississippi this fall for a bear hunt. The people will draw a sigh of relief when it is known that the state will not be treated to a visit by a nigger equality president. His presence in Mississippi would not be taken as an honor or compliment to the state. We are glad that Mr. Roosevelt cannot come.*

This editorial may stem from the fact that on October 16, 1901, after moving to the White House, Teddy and his family invited Booker T. Washington to dine with them there. Booker T. Washington, the founder of what is now Tuskegee University, was an early activist for civil rights and the first Black man ever to dine at the White House. The dinner angered the whole South, and it seemed that almost every southern newspaper and politician weighed in on the subject. Governor of Georgia Allen Candler stated, "No self-respecting man can ally himself with the President, after

Booker T. Washington, a prominent civil rights leader and former slave, was the first African American to be invited to dine at the White House. *Library of Congress.*

what has occurred. No Southerner can respect any white man who would eat with a negro." As usual, Teddy was more concerned with doing what he believed was right than what the press thought of him.

With a great desire to kill a black bear, Teddy changed his mind and requested that the hunt be planned in secret to keep the number of hunters to a minimum. Major George Helm, the same Major Helm who had employed Holt to act as a jail guard, was asked to book Holt's services for the soon-to-be famous hunt. Helm told Collier, "If you can get things ready in a month and not let anybody know what you're doing, President Roosevelt will go hunting with us." With his usual gusto, Holt began to scout for the perfect hunting spot and campground for what was to be the most famous hunter he had been able to guide up until that point in his career. Settling on Smedes, Mississippi, Holt and his men began to manually clear the canebrake for campsites and shooting lanes. Clearing canebrake is hard and intense labor, which must be done carefully to keep the workers from getting cut by the sharp edges of the cane. As usual, even at the age of fifty-six, Holt outworked many of the much younger men he employed.

Not only did Holt believe that the area around Smedes was President Roosevelt's best chance to bring down a black bear, but it was also home to a very isolated train station used to load and haul cotton along the rails. The station would allow the president to get close to the campsite as quickly and painlessly as possible. On November 13, 1902, Teddy stepped from the platform into the chilly November day, dressed in a blue flannel shirt, corduroy coat, brown slouch hat, riding trousers and leather leggings. In the crook of his arm, Teddy was carrying his Winchester .40-90 and his fringed buckskin jacket. Hundreds of people, mostly African Americans, were crowded around the train station hoping to get a glimpse of the commander in chief.

CHAPTER 14

THE TEDDY BEAR IS BORN

Much to the president's annoyance, the train had been packed with reporters, stenographers and other hangers-on. Teddy Roosevelt, personable as always, walked up to Holt, hand extended, and introduced himself. Holt was pleased by the gesture, as many Whites would never have shaken a Black man's hand during this time. In an interview about the experience, Holt stated that Roosevelt said to him, "So dis is Holt, de guide. I hyar you's er a great bear hunter." The compliment must have pleased Holt, who took pride in his ability to provide his clients with a good hunt that ended with a kill.

Adhering to the president's wishes to keep the number of people at his campsite very small, two guards, Ben Johnson and Freeman Wallace, were posted on the road into the camp, armed with repeating rifles. Two Black armed guards on the road to the president's camp was not a welcomed prospect in rural Mississippi. Riding atop a black horse, Teddy was followed by the rest of his party on horseback, except for Mr. Fish and Mr. Dickinson, who were too fat to mount horses. The two overweight men climbed aboard a buckboard drawn by two mules and rode into camp. Arriving at four o'clock in the afternoon, the president and his party began to settle into camp. Per his request, word was spread to the camp that while on his hunting trip, the president preferred to be called colonel, the rank he achieved while in the Spanish-American War.

The pressure to get the president a bear must have been intense, but Holt, with his usual self-confidence, started the hunt at eight o'clock on Friday morning. Directing Colonel Roosevelt to a blind, where he thought the president would have the greatest chance of killing a bear, Holt released his dogs. Before long, the pack of dogs had hit a scent trail and were fast on the heels of the hunt's first bear. Unfortunately, the bear was running away from where Colonel Roosevelt and Mr. Huger Foote were sitting waiting for a shot. After hours of waiting for the bear, Colonel Roosevelt and Mr. Foote grew hungry and returned to camp to eat some lunch.

With Colonel Roosevelt back in camp, Holt's dogs turned the bear around, and it headed back to where Roosevelt had been. Running past Roosevelt's blind, the bear went down into the water, and a fight ensued between it and the dogs. Worried about his dogs, Holt dismounted, pulled his rifle from its scabbard and charged into the water. Wielding his rifle, Holt hit the bear over the head, dizzying it. Lassoing the bear, he tied it to a willow tree and waited for the president to return.

In the *Topeka State Journal*, Holt gave a firsthand account of the incident.

> *When my dogs did run dat b'ar down he went down in a mud hole, and it was kinder thick and hard to get at so I stood round and didn't shoot, 'cause I wanted the colonel to hurry up and come in behind me so he could kill the first one. I tried my best to get dat big b'ar to tree, but he wouldn't, so I thought he was jes' goin to get the best of my pack, so I hit him with the butt of my gun and then thrown my lasso 'bout his neck and made him fast to a willer tree.*

When Colonel Roosevelt finally, arrived Holt told him, "Shoot de b'ar, colonel, he's tied."

In Holt's own words, "'Scuse me,' says Colonel Roosevelt laffin' at the b'ar all tied up dar nice and snug. 'Scuse me,' ses he, 'dat's too easy.'"

When Roosevelt refused to kill the bear, Holt suggested that Mr. Parker, one of the men in the hunting party, kill the bear with a knife. Following Holt's instructions, Mr. Parker quickly killed the bear, making it the first kill of the hunt.

After Mr. Parker killed the bear, Holt told the president, "Colonel, you watch me close and you sho'ly get a b'ar."

The president laughed and said, "All right, Holt. I'll keep an eye on you."

Taking the bear back to camp, the men dressed it and hung it in a tree. After lunch, the hunting resumed, and one of the hunting parties brought bear number two into the camp. The second bear, Holt claimed, was much smaller than the first. Disappointed but not defeated, Colonel Roosevelt was sure that he would kill a bear the next day.

"Drawing the Line in Mississippi" is Clifford Berryman's rendering of Roosevelt's famous bear hunt. The man in the background represents Holt Collier, despite appearing as a White man. *Library of Congress.*

Up early the next morning, a Saturday, the hunting party decided that a different strategy was needed to get Colonel Roosevelt a chance at a bear. This time, Colonel Roosevelt would be mounted, chasing Holt's large pack of dogs, crashing through the canebrakes and swamps. Sitting astride Josh Christian's black mare, Roosevelt cut an impressive figure among the members of the hunting party. Roosevelt's joy and enthusiasm were felt throughout the camp. That morning, Holt was mounted on old Frank, whom he had been riding for many years, when they released the dogs. Impressed with Colonel Roosevelt's skills in the saddle, Holt said, "Of course she ain't no saddler, an' she lopes hard, but Col. Roosevelt was no a holdin' back for nothin' and he rode hard after b'ars, shu." Despite hunting for hours, crashing through canebrakes and riding hard, Colonel Roosevelt was empty-handed when he rode back into camp before sunset.

On Sunday, with most of the hunting party being religious, they decided not to hunt, spending much of the day in quiet reflection. The camp was

Roosevelt in the saddle, ready for the hunt. He was a superb rider who relished being in the saddle for many hours. *Courtesy of* Delta Magazine.

peaceful, with the president and other members of the party walking through the woods, enjoying nature. According to the *Topeka State Journal*, the evening meal was the principal event of the day. As the men gathered around a rough pine board table, the smell of bear paws and possum cooked in sweet potatoes made their mouth water. Roosevelt stated that his favorite part of the meal was the roasted possum in sweet potatoes. Having eaten wild game on many occasions, the president was right at home as they enjoyed their meal and swapped hunting stories as they ate. According to the paper, Roosevelt was enjoying the tranquility of the hunting trip being that it was his first vacation away from the White House since being sworn in as president.

Holt, determined for the president to bag a bear, began the third day of the hunt early on Monday, November 17. Holt and Colonel Roosevelt had very little luck until around two o'clock, when Holt's dogs scented a bear. The dogs chased the bear for an hour with President Roosevelt and Holt fast on its trail. Finally, around three o'clock, the bear broke from the dogs and crossed the river, never to be seen again. Roosevelt laughed and said, "I expect we aren't going to get a bear this trip." Having no luck, the president and Holt rode back to camp to prepare for the last day of hunting.

The last day was cool and cloudy, and the dogs worked as hard as usual, but luck, once again, eluded the president. When the hunt was over, they returned and quickly began to break down camp. Disappointment hung over the camp, more from the hunters who were hoping to get the president a bear than the president himself. Even empty-handed, Roosevelt was pleased with the outcome, having enjoyed his time in the great outdoors. Roosevelt told Holt, "This was a delightful place and I hate to leave it." As a souvenir, Roosevelt took the skull of the bear that Mr. Parker had killed back with him to the White House.

About the president leaving, Holt said, "I wants to tell you dat I hated mightily to see de president go away, and so did all de odders down hyar. I kin only say day he's the finest from de No'th dat I ever met."

At the time of the hunt, Collier, in his fifties, wore a small beard with a mustache and had the eyesight of a much younger man. His legs were also as strong as a man half his age, allowing him to stay in the woods all day without resting. The hunt had claimed two of Holt's dogs, and a third was dying. The 1902 hunt became more than just a hunt; it became a subject of national interest, and it made Holt Collier a household name throughout the South.

In Roosevelt's refusal to shoot the lassoed bear, Americans saw a sense of fair play, especially after Clifford Berryman, the well-known political cartoonist, immortalized the incident in a political cartoon titled "Drawing the Line in Mississippi." The cartoon pictured Roosevelt dressed in his hunting clothes, back turned to a small black bear, clutching a rifle in his right hand, with his left hand extended behind him in a form of rejection. The bear, dragged by a nondescript person who is supposed to represent Holt Collier, is being pulled by a rope around its neck. The bear in the cartoon is portrayed as a small cub, while the real-life bear was a grown adult who was large enough to kill one of Holt's dogs.

Seeing Berryman's cartoon, Morris Michtom, a Brooklyn toyshop owner, and his wife, Rose, cut a piece of plush velvet, stuffed it in the shape of a bear and sewed button eyes on their new creation. They dubbed their creation Teddy's Bear and placed it in the front window of their shop. Fearing that his use of the president's name would anger the most powerful man in America, Michtom mailed the prototype to the White House and asked permission to call his creation the Teddy Bear. Roosevelt replied, "I

Pictured is an early teddy bear factory. The toy quickly became one of the greatest-selling toys in the United States. *Library of Congress.*

don't think my name will help, but you are welcome to use it." Roosevelt could not have been more wrong, as teddy bears have become one of the greatest-selling toys of all time. Michtom's small toyshop eventually evolved into the Ideal Toy Company, which went on to sell millions of teddy bears throughout the world. Without a patent, the teddy bear was copied again and again by different competitors, but the Roosevelt family always credited the Michtoms with the original stuffed bear. The original Teddy Bear, sent to Roosevelt, is now on display at the Smithsonian in Washington, D.C.

Chapter 15

ROOSEVELT ARRIVES IN LOUISIANA

The president was so impressed with Holt Collier's abilities and the tranquility of the Mississippi Delta that he told Holt he would try to return within three years. After returning to Washington, D.C., Roosevelt, engaged in the business of the presidency, realized that his goal of returning to Mississippi in three years just wasn't feasible. In the meantime, Holt's life went on much the same as before as he continued to train dogs and guide hunts. At the request of many prominent White planters, Holt began to teach their children how to hunt, track and ride. As the years passed and the black bear population continued to dwindle, Holt found it harder and harder to make money as a hunting guide. Eventually, with little income, he turned to the government for help. In April 1906, Holt applied for a Confederate servant pension. Never having shaken his gambling habit or saved much money, Holt was borderline destitute.

In a letter to the pension board, Holt made it clear that he was unable to support himself with his current line of work. Despite the efforts of Howell Hinds, Holt had never learned to read or write, which meant that someone else had to fill out the paperwork for it to be sent to the pension board. The paperwork stated that Holt had acted as Lieutenant Tom Hinds's servant during the war and that he had been wounded during the Battle of Shiloh. Holt also had another reason to file for assistance, as he was married for the last time on April 24, 1904. Having turned fifty-eight years old, he married Frances Perkins, who was thirty-two years younger than Holt. A person of exceptional beauty, she brought a child called Toots to the marriage. Holt's other wives have faded into obscurity. The pension board approved Holt's pension, allowing him a steady source of income, albeit a very modest sum.

Meanwhile, during his three-year hiatus from hunting in the South, President Roosevelt ran for his first full term in office in 1904. His opponent for the presidency was Democrat Alton B. Parker, a lawyer, who had been serving on the New York Supreme Court of Appeals as chief justice since 1898. As a Democrat, Parker won thirteen southern states, only garnering 140 electoral votes. Even though it had been three years since Booker T. Washington dined in the White House, it seemed that the South still begrudged President Roosevelt dining with an African American. Roosevelt did not need the support of southern democrats, as he went on to win in a landslide, receiving 336 electoral votes. It would not be his last time running for the presidential office, but it would be his most successful.

Never having forgotten Holt Collier and the enjoyable experience of hunting in the Mississippi Delta, President Roosevelt returned to the South in 1907, but this time he would be hunting in Louisiana. Holt, who had spent much time in Louisiana's swamps chasing black bears, would be called back into action. At the time of the hunt, Holt was sixty-one years old but still a capable hunter. Arriving at Stamboul, Louisiana, by train, President Roosevelt, determined to keep the hunt much quieter than his 1902 excursion, quickly mounted his horse and rode straight to camp. Holt, who had traveled to Greenville to round up his hunting dogs, was not in the camp when the president arrived. Roosevelt's hunting party included Dr. Hugh Miller, Dr. Presley Rixey, Dr. Alexander Lambert, John Parker, Major Amacker and John McIlhenny. The legendary bear hunter, Ben Lilly had also been invited to help with the hunt.

Benjamin Vernon Lilly came into the world on a cold New Year's Eve in 1856, in Wilcox County, Alabama, the oldest of seven siblings. Lilly's family moved to Mississippi, where he spent most of his childhood. Coming from a long line of metalworkers, Ben learned the art of blacksmithing from his father, who shod horses, fixed farm implements and made eighteen-inch knives that were carried by General Nathan Bedford Forrest's troops during the Civil War. Moving to Louisiana, Ben opened his blacksmith shop, where he also repaired farm equipment, shod horses and created Lilly knives. At five feet, nine inches tall and 180 pounds, Ben was exceptionally strong and capable of lifting an anvil with one hand. Many people claim he could heave a five-hundred-pound cotton bale above his head and carry it. His ability to run and his speed also added to his legend. His persistence

Ben Lilly in his golden years, painted with one of his beloved hunting dogs. He and Holt Collier achieved fame for being tough and adventurous hunters. *Courtesy of* Sporting Classics Daily.

was widely known, as he would often chase game for twenty-four hours without eating or sleeping.

By the time he met Roosevelt, Ben was living more like a nineteenth-century pioneer than a twentieth-century American citizen. Having abandoned living indoors, Ben dressed like a mountain man. Writing about the first time he met Lilly, Roosevelt stated,

> *The morning Lilly joined us in camp, he had come on foot through the thick woods, followed by his two dogs, and had neither eaten nor drunk for twenty-four hours; for he did not like to drink swamp water. It had rained hard throughout the night, and he had no shelter, no rubber coat, nothing but the clothes he was wearing, the ground was too wet for him to lie on, so he perched in a crooked tree in the beating rain, much as if he had been a wild turkey.*

Roosevelt also, with profound respect, stated that he had never seen another man who was so immune to hardship and fatigue as Ben Lilly.

Ben Lilly, like Holt, had chased and hunted bears and mountain lions throughout many states, gaining a name for himself as a wonderful shot and a capable guide. As is the case with many hunters, Ben preferred certain guns, using a Winchester 1894 .30-30 to hunt mountain lions and black bears and a Winchester .33 when hunting the much tougher grizzly bear. Much like Holt, Ben also had a deep fondness for his hunting dogs. Ben paid homage to his favorite hunting dog when it died near Sapillo Creek, New Mexico, in 1925, by inscribing the box it was buried in with this epitaph, "Here lies Crook, a bear and lion dog that helped kill 210 bear and 426 lions since 1911, owned by B.V. Lilly." Having great confidence in Holt's and Ben's abilities, the president was convinced that he would bag a black bear this time.

In September, before the hunt began, Holt had arrived in Louisiana to make sure that the hunting grounds were prepped to provide the president with the best hunt possible. The Louisiana canebrakes, which were much thicker than ones in Mississippi, would require much more work before the hunt began. At ten to fifteen feet tall, the canebrakes were often blown together, creating narrow, impenetrable lanes among the cane. Using a double-edged, straight-blade knife, Holt chopped down lanes for the dogs and horses to travel through during the hunt. The work would have been hard for a man half Holt's age, but the sixty-one-year-old was determined to provide President Roosevelt with the best hunting experience possible. The Louisiana canebrakes, unlike those in Mississippi, were still home to a great number of black bears. They were also home to wild boar, a small number of panthers, whitetail deer and bobcats. During his time in the canebrakes, Holt spent a large amount of time scouting for tracks, scat and other signs of bears.

With his prep work finished, Holt traveled to Greenville, gathered his twenty-two hunting dogs and arrived back in Louisiana on October 7. The quiet of the camp was broken by the yelping of Holt's large pack of hunting dogs. The president and Holt, who shared mutual respect, were happy to see each other once again. Settling into camp, Holt prepared his equipment for the upcoming hunt. Newspaper reporters were very interested in seeing which of the two famed hunters, Ben Lilly or Holt Collier, would be the first to get President Roosevelt a shot at a bear. There was also much interest in which legendary hunter would bring down the most game during the hunt. Lilly versus Collier was portrayed as a friendly rivalry in the press.

Having arrived on a Saturday, Roosevelt, as was his custom, did not hunt on Sunday. Even if he had wanted to hunt, Ben Lilly would have refused, as he was, according to all accounts, a religious fanatic. Ironically, as religious as Ben was, he had grown so accustomed to living outside that his two wives had procured divorce proceedings against him, claiming abandonment. Lilly began the hunt with a spot of bad luck, as his old hunting dog Joe injured his paw during the train ride to Louisiana, incapacitating him for the hunt. With a multitude of hunting dogs in the party, old Joe's inability to hunt was not a major setback, and the hunt could continue as planned. On that Sunday, President Roosevelt did not attend church but spent time in his tent reading and meditating. The president's tent was a fourteen-by-sixteen-foot box tent with a wooden floor, furnished with a bed, a rough writing desk and a few chairs. Roosevelt deemed the accommodations excellent, as he had stayed in much less comfortable conditions hundreds of times throughout his rustic pursuits.

Weeks before the hunt, the area had been experiencing a severe drought, making the ground as hard as pavement. The condition of the ground would pose a problem for Holt's and the other hunters' dogs, as their paws would become so sore that they might be unable to hunt. A bear hunt without dogs is not impossible, but the advantage of having a great pack of bear dogs could not be underestimated. Luckily, when Roosevelt arrived at camp, the skies opened and the rains poured down, softening the ground and making the conditions almost ideal for the hunt. Unfortunately, the rain caused the humidity to soar, making it almost unbearable. However, neither rain, shine nor humidity would stop them from hunting, and they spent Sunday night preparing for the first day of the hunt.

CHAPTER 16

ROOSEVELT GETS HIS BEAR

T he hunt began in earnest on Monday, October 8, with both Holt and Lilly leading the way into the canebrakes. Both famous hunters had pledged to help the president kill a bear before his trip came to an end. On the first day of the hunt, Ben Lilly said, "If the President's aim with his shotgun is as good as it is with the 'big stick'"—referring to Roosevelt's foreign policy of "walking softly and carrying a big stick"—"there is certain to be a bear strung outside of the White House tent this evening." Unfortunately for the president, he was unable to show off his superior marksmanship, as the hunting party never even crossed paths with a bear that day. Under the circumstances and on Holt's advice, they decided that the best thing they could do was move to a better location.

Pulling up stakes, the hunting party moved fourteen miles away, setting up camp near Bear Lake. The move would be a good one, but it did require them to abandon the area that Holt and others had worked so hard to clear. Luckily, the party found a small hunting shack, where the president took up residence. The change of hunting grounds worked, and on the first morning in the new location, Holt's dogs struck a bear's scent trail. Running, yelping and crashing through the canebrakes, the dogs eventually lost the bear's scent. During the day's hunt, a bear was killed, but unfortunately for Roosevelt, he did not fire the fatal shot. As darkness fell, they retired to the camp to plan for the next day. In keeping with Jim Crow laws, every night, two campfires were built, one for the White hunters and the other for the Black guides. While many of the White hunters stayed around their campfire, Roosevelt, still referred to as "colonel" on this hunt, would mosey over to the guides' campfire nightly, swapping hunting stories with them.

One of the most dangerous moments of the hunt was when a wild boar, referred to as Hogzilla in many articles, almost killed Doctor Rixey. In his article "Hogs Roman and Boar Hunting, Ancient and Modern," published on January 7, 1935, Charles Knapp described the attack.

> *One pair* [of tusks] *found by Governor Parker measured seven and five-eighths inches, taken from the boar that attacked Doctor Rixey, personal physician to President Theodore Roosevelt, while Teddy was on a hunting expedition. This infuriated devil might have slain Doctor Rixey, if Holt Collier, the celebrated Negro hunter, had not thrown himself between them, grappled the beast, and stabbed him to death. Doctor Rixey, I am told, now had his tusks as a souvenir of luck.*

On October 16, Holt's dogs cornered a black bear, and a terrible fight ensued. When Holt finally arrived, two of his dogs were in danger of being killed by the very angry bear. Raising his rifle, Holt had no choice but to kill the bear to save the lives of his dogs. Holt was disappointed that he had killed a bear before Colonel Roosevelt. The bear was quickly dressed, skinned and hung outside the president's lodgings. At the request of Colonel Roosevelt, the bear's hide was taken into Stamboul to be tanned and sent to the White House.

With time running out in the hunt, Roosevelt voiced his concerns to Holt: "Holt, I haven't got but one or two more days. What am I going to do? I haven't killed a bear."

Ever the optimist, Holt replied, "Cunnel, ef you let me manage the hunt you'll sho' kill one to-morrow. One of 'em got away to-day that you ought to have killed."

Holt decided that Roosevelt, who had been sitting at a stand much of the time, needed to change tactics. Hanging back with Clive Metcalfe, Roosevelt waited while the other hunters tore off through the canebrakes to roust out a bear. Running across a hot trail, the dogs began to chase a bear in the wrong direction. Finally, the bear turned back toward the president, and when he and Metcalfe heard the baying of the hounds, they mounted up and spurred their horses onward into the canebrakes. When Roosevelt heard the dogs drawing near, he dismounted, tore off his coat and ran into the canebrakes. Spotting the bear, followed by the dogs, Roosevelt raised his Winchester and squeezed off a shot. Wounded, the bear, determined to survive, turned on

Wild hogs, as we call them in Mississippi, can be very deadly, as is evident from the sharp tusks protruding from this hog's mouth. *Courtesy of Regan McFerrin Mitchell.*

the dogs. Before the bear could hurt one of the hunting dogs, Roosevelt sent another round between its shoulders, breaking its neck. The rest of the hunting party came charging toward the sound of gunfire, where they found Roosevelt smiling his large toothy grin. The president was so excited he embraced some of the other hunters.

Following the hunt, while at Leo Shields's residency, President Roosevelt summed up the hunt by saying,

> *We got three bears, six deer, one wild turkey, twelve squirrels, one duck, one 'possum, and one wild cat. We ate them all except the wild cat, and there were times when we almost felt we could eat it.*

When asked about the satisfaction of the hunt, he said, "Yes, we got three bears. All that we saw, and I think a pretty good record. I am perfectly satisfied." The president also gave his opinion on the camp food, stating that the possum he ate was excellent, second only to bear liver. According to the president, swimming had also been a daily routine for the hunting party. "The water was fine," he said, "and I did not have the fear of alligators that some seem to have." The Shreveport newspaper reported that the president declared his health was wonderful and his appetite was equally good. During the hunt, except for when it was raining, he had been in the saddle almost every day from dawn till dusk.

On October 21, President Roosevelt left Leo Shields's home and crossed the river to Vicksburg, Mississippi. Escorted by one hundred committee members, Roosevelt was met by Mayor Griffith and General Stephen D. Lee. As they rode toward the Vicksburg National Military Park, cheers went up from onlookers crowding the street to get a glimpse of the former Rough Rider. When the carriage came to a stop at the corner of Cherry and Clay Streets, Roosevelt was greeted by several hundred Confederate and Union soldiers, with whom he gladly shook hands. Governor Vardaman was noticeably absent, as he had been known to harshly criticize the president on more than one occasion. After visiting the cemetery, the carriage proceeded onward toward the courthouse square, where President Roosevelt gave a rousing speech. Immediately after his last words were spoken, he was whisked away, boarding a special train that departed for Memphis.

Two months after the hunt, on December 24, 1907, President Roosevelt wrote a letter to the great African American hunter.

Right: Governor of Mississippi James Vardaman disagreed with President Roosevelt on many political and social ideologies. He shunned Roosevelt when he came to Mississippi in 1907. *Courtesy of Mississippi History Timeline.*

Opposite: Holt Collier holding the 1886 Winchester .45-70 that was given to him by President Roosevelt. *Courtesy of the Great Delta Bear Affair Website.*

> *Holt Collier:*
> *I am very much obliged for the cup and the buck's foot. It will be an interesting memento of the hunt. Glad you liked the gun.*
> *Wishing you a merry Christmas and a happy New Year,*
> *Sincerely yours,*
> *Theodore Roosevelt*
>
> *Mr. Holt Collier*
> *c/o Clive Metcalfe, Esq.*
> *Wilcainski, Mississippi*

The gun Roosevelt was referring to in the letter was a Winchester 1886 lever action .45-70. Following the hunt, President Roosevelt had ordered three of the rifles sent to Holt Collier, Clive Metcalfe and Harley Metcalfe, one apiece. The Winchester 1886 model .45-70 was one of the finest and most powerful rifles at the time. The rifle would have been a fine prize for any hunter, but being a gift from the president himself made it an especially prized possession. The gift was also a representation of the bond between the four men.

In commemoration of his hunt, President Roosevelt invited his hunting companions to dine at the White House. Roosevelt was thrilled with the success of the dinner, which became known as the "Teddy Bear dinner." Holt and Ben Lilly both politely declined their invitations. Had Holt accepted the invitation and dined at the White House, there is little doubt that the South would have been angered once again by the president dining with an African American. When asked why he had declined, Holt replied,

> *The President wanted me to go to Washington with him, and lots o' negroes aroun' here thought I was a mighty big fool for not goin'. But I didn't have any friends in Washington, an' I couldn't hunt up there. So, I thought the best thing for me to do would be to stay right here among my people.*

Serving out the rest of his term, President Roosevelt decided not to run for a third. On leaving office, he endorsed Vice President William Howard Taft as his replacement. With Roosevelt's endorsement, Taft easily defeated Democrat William Jennings Bryan in the 1908 election. Much to Roosevelt's disappointment, Taft refused to use the bully pulpit and was much more moderate on many issues than the former president had hoped. So, following Taft's first term in office, Roosevelt decided that he would run for office again in the 1912 presidential election. As the incumbent, Taft received the Republican nomination, forcing Roosevelt to run as a third-party candidate. The newly formed Bull Moose Party, formerly the Progressive Party, was hoping to effect social and political change, nominating Teddy Roosevelt as their candidate at their convention in August 1912.

Hitting the campaign trail, Roosevelt was filled with a renewed spirit, and he began campaigning with his usual gusto. Surprisingly, while Roosevelt was campaigning in Milwaukee, Wisconsin, on October 14, 1912, John Flammang Schrank stepped from the crowd, aimed a .32-caliber pistol

President Roosevelt is pictured with his family, who were affectionately referred to as the "White House Gang." *Library of Congress.*

at Roosevelt's heart and fired. Luckily for the former president, the bullet was slowed by his glasses case, a fifty-page speech and his coat. With his usual bravado, Roosevelt pulled his bloodstained speech from his pocket and quipped, "You see, it takes more than one bullet to kill a bull moose." After delivering an hour-long speech, Roosevelt was taken to the hospital, where the doctors decided that surgery to remove the bullet would be more dangerous than leaving it in place. Roosevelt carried the bullet with him for the rest of his life. As third-party candidates often do, Roosevelt split the Republican vote, allowing Woodrow Wilson to win a decisive victory.

After losing the election, the fifty-five-year-old Roosevelt set out on an Amazonian adventure that would nearly take his life. Along with his son Kermit, he explored an uncharted river in South America, which took over seven months. While on the trip, Roosevelt contracted a terrible case of malaria. After falling ill, he cut his leg on a rock, and the wound became badly infected. The infection was so serious that emergency surgery, performed on a riverbank, was needed to save the former president's leg. During his ordeal, Roosevelt lost a quarter of his body weight and was lucky to make it out of the jungle alive. Returning to New York in May 1914, Roosevelt walked down his ship's gangplank and was greeted by a group of friends and admirers. The Amazonian adventure would be his last, as malaria and infection had taken a heavy toll on Roosevelt.

Despite his health beginning to fail, Roosevelt approached President Woodrow Wilson when America entered World War I and asked if he could organize a military unit to fight the Germans. Wilson, of course, refused Roosevelt for two reasons: the first reason was that if Roosevelt was successful, it would inflame Roosevelt's popularity, making him an even more powerful opponent in the next presidential election, and the second reason was that if Wilson agreed and Roosevelt was killed, many people would resent Wilson for allowing him to go fight. Relegated to touring the country, Roosevelt helped raise awareness of the war and the need for Americans to buy war bonds. Teddy wasn't alone in his zeal for his country, as his six children pitched in to help with the war effort. His youngest son, Quentin, a combat pilot, was shot down and killed behind enemy lines on July 14, 1918. After the death of his son, President Roosevelt was never the same, and the lion of the White House went out not with a roar but a whisper on January 6, 1919. Doctors believed that he died from a pulmonary embolism. He never lived to see the end of the war and the Allied victory over the Central Powers.

CHAPTER 17

HOLT'S TWILIGHT YEARS

Despite being twelve years older than Roosevelt, Holt would outlive the former president by seventeen years. Holt, who was sixty-one years old at the time of the 1907 bear hunt, had plenty of life left in him. Like Roosevelt, he would never be satisfied to sit idly by while other men sought out adventure. When Roosevelt headed back to Washington, Holt continued to hunt black bears, despite their declining populations. During that time, his relationship with the Metcalfe family continued to grow as he took young Albert, Clive's son, under his wing and taught him how to hunt. One of the most memorable moments of Albert's life occurred while hunting with Holt when he killed a large black bear at age ten. The bear was massive, weighing around three hundred pounds, and for Holt, young Albert's experience brought memories flooding back of when he killed his first black bear at the age of ten.

Feeling his years, Holt gave up his days of rambling and moved into a permanent dwelling in Greenville, Mississippi. This act of domestication was strange for Holt, who had spent most of his life sleeping in tents or under the stars. Frequent visitors, hoping to catch a glimpse of the famous hunter, often stayed long hours at Holt's house as he regaled them with stories of his battles with dangerous bears, panthers and hogs. Saddened by Roosevelt's death, Holt admitted that he had always hoped to take Colonel Roosevelt on one more adventure, but it would never happen. Holt said about the president's death, "Put an end to my huntin' wid Roosevelt. I still got de gun he done give me!" The death of the former president hung heavily over Holt, as it did the whole nation.

Even in his twilight years, Roosevelt could not forget his famous bear hunt as merchandise of all sorts was sold commemorating his adventure in Mississippi. *Courtesy of Wikimedia Commons.*

As Holt's life changed, so did the city of Greenville. The city, which had once been the cultural and business epicenter for the county's sprawling plantations, now served as a vital location for former slaves, who worked as sharecroppers. After the war, Greenville became a racial melting pot with a significant number of Jews, Asians, Italians, Whites and African Americans living in the city limits toward the end of the nineteenth century. In 1875, the city's diversity shined as its citizens elected the city's first Jewish mayor, Leopold Wilczinski. At the same time, Jewish businesses began to pop up along the streets of Greenville, adding a diversity of stores to the growing city. By 1910, Greenville's population numbered over ten thousand, and the city was thriving by the time Holt moved into the city limits.

Greenville and the rest of the Delta, with its large African American population, served as somewhat of a safe place for many African Americans. Given the Delta's very small White population, the KKK had been unable to establish a foothold there, but at the beginning of the twentieth century, they made a push to start a Klavern (a local branch of the KKK) in Greenville. It was Leroy Percy, a state politician, who was responsible for helping keep the Klan out of Greenville and Washington County. Despite viewing African Americans as inferior, Percy believed that all people should be afforded the same rights, regardless of their race. His motivations were not entirely unselfish, as he owned a large plantation, which relied heavily on Black laborers. By keeping race relations civil in the Delta, Percy ensured that his workers would continue to make money for his plantation. Whatever his motivation, his efforts to keep the Klan at bay were very effective.

When the KKK tried to gain a foothold on March 1, 1922, with a recruitment meeting in Greenville, Percy charged into the fray, giving a fiery speech that reminded the crowd of how much good Jewish businessmen had done for the city of Greenville. Percy then verbally attacked the KKK recruitment officer "Colonel" Joseph Camp's ludicrous Catholic conspiracies and Camp's use of a fake military title. Percy finished his speech by saying, "Friends let this Klan go somewhere else where it will not do the harm it will in this community. Let them sow dissension in some community less united than is ours." The crowd, which Percy had packed with his supporters, broke into a thunderous round of applause. After Percy's speech, "Colonel" Camp left Greenville, his tail tucked between his legs and the Klan repulsed.

With the town of Greenville safe from the Klan, African Americans, including Holt, settled into a comfortable routine. Holt, with his sweeping white mustache and pointy beard, could be spotted strolling easily along Greenville's newly paved streets. Even when his back was turned, people could spot Holt, because he still wore the wide-brimmed hat from his Texas Cavalry days. His front porch was often frequented by the city's children and adults alike as he regaled them with tales of his life as a slave, Confederate soldier and professional hunter. There is little doubt that Holt's ability for storytelling was developed during the countless hours he spent around a campfire.

Greenville and Holt were tested to their limit in 1927 when the Mississippi River overflowed its banks. The Great Flood of '27, as it became known, was one of the worst natural disasters in American history. Henry Waring Ball of Greenville wrote in his diary,

> *The worst Good Friday I ever saw. A night of incessant storms, wind, lightning, thunder, and torrents of rain. Raining constantly all this morning, none of us slept much. A day too dark and stormy to go to church or even out of doors. Discomfort. Flowers and plants beaten to the earth, little half-drowned chickens in baskets in the kitchen, house leaking in many places. Everybody in a bad humor except Jane, the cook. River appallingly high, and the levees in very precarious condition. Too dark to write, another big storm coming—noon.*

Ball later reported in his diary that Greenville received ten inches of rain in one day. Greenville's fifteen thousand inhabitants were in danger as the water levels continued to rise. North of Greenville, the Miller Bend and the Mounds Landing levees were areas of great concern. If those two levees broke, the city itself would be flooded. Rushing to the levees, citizens of Greenville began to fill and pile sandbags up as fast as they could along the top of the levees. Regardless of their efforts, the Mounds Landing levee broke on April 21, 1927, sending the muddy, swirling waters of the mighty river down the streets of Greenville.

Holt, a man who was always prepared, had lived by the raging river for most of his life and was one of the few people in Greenville who lived in a two-story house. Taking refuge on the second floor, Holt and his wife survived upstairs for four months. Luckily, the elderly Holt and Frances were able to rely on the charity of their neighbors and friends to help feed them during the flood. By the time the flood ended, twenty-three thousand square miles of land were submerged, 250 people had been killed and hundreds of thousands of people had lost their homes. Water, clothing and food were

Two African American men in the middle of Greenville, Mississippi, during the Great Flood of 1927. *Courtesy of BlackPast.*

also scarce or nonexistent for 750,000 African Americans. As the waters receded, Holt's house was still standing but severely damaged.

With houses, fields and prospects destroyed, many African America moved north looking for work, and Greenville's population dropped as many of the city's inhabitants joined in the Great Migration. Remaining in Greenville, Holt fell into a deep depression as he watched his friends leave and he was forced to deal with the flood damage to his house. Feeble and unable to work, Holt depended on Frances's income as an occasional housekeeper. Luckily, his Confederate servant's pension was also renewed. Amazingly, in 1928, Holt was officially recognized by the State of Mississippi as a Confederate veteran. With the recognition, he began to receive a veteran's pension, which was more than his previous pension.

In 1931, Holt suffered the worst blow of his life when Frances, his wife of twenty-seven years, died on October 9 of a cerebral hemorrhage. As a man who had finally found marital bliss on his third try, Holt was devastated by the loss of his wife. Left with his stepson, Toots, Holt continued to live in the same house, mourning Frances for the rest of his life. Holt's worst fear had come to fruition. He had outlived almost everyone he ever cared about: his parents, the Metcalfe brothers, President Roosevelt, Howell Hinds, several of his siblings, friends and his precious Frances. Death had not yet taken Holt, but he spiraled even deeper into a state of depression.

In the few years he had left, Holt remained nostalgic, sharing tales from his younger days with anyone who would listen. Unable to take care of himself any longer, Holt, at ninety, moved into the home of Sarah Williams. Williams ran a nursing home out of her home, caring for the elderly and

This is one of the last known photos of Holt Collier. *Courtesy of www. holtcollier.com.*

infirm. Bedridden and under the care of Dr. Otis H. Beck, Holt passed away at 10:10 a.m. on Wednesday, August 1, 1936, at the age of ninety.

The man Teddy Roosevelt referred to as "the greatest hunter he ever knew" had witnessed an amazing number of changes to the world during his ninety years. He had fought in the Civil War, witnessed slavery being struck down by the Thirteenth Amendment, seen the invention of the incandescent light bulb and lived through World War I and part of the Great Depression. Holt was buried on August 3, 1936, at Live Oak Cemetery in Greenville. He was buried within miles of where he spent much of his life, chasing bears, making memories and building his legacy.

Right: Holt Collier was immortalized in this beautiful bronze sculpture created by artist Jay Warren. *Courtesy of Jay Warren.*

Below: The Holt Collier National Wildlife Refuge is the only NWR named after an African American in the United States. *Courtesy of the Heritage Post.*

The legacy of Holt Collier lives on, not only in the memories of his great hunts but also in his thirst for life. In 2004, the U.S. Wildlife Service honored Holt by naming a national wildlife refuge in the Mississippi Delta after him. The Holt Collier National Wildlife Refuge is the only national wildlife refuge in the United States named for an African American. Today, the U.S. Wildlife Service is making a concerted effort to reverse much of the damage that has been done to the swamps and forests of the Delta. The organization is also striving to repopulate Mississippi's black bear population. The Mississippi Department of Wildlife reported in June 2022 that there are well over one hundred black bears residing in the state, and with continued conservation efforts, the numbers will continue to rise. Wherever there is a bear in Mississippi, a canebrake or a swamp, there will be a trace of the legendary bear hunter Holt Collier.

BIBLIOGRAPHY

Abilene (KS) Weekly Reflector. September 11, 1902. Library of Congress. https://www.loc.gov/resource/sn84029386/1902-09-11/ed:1/.

Adams, Michael C. C. "Seeing the Elephant: On the Civil War Battlefields." HistoryNet. February 21, 2017. https://www.historynet.com/seeing-the-elephant-on-the-civil-war-battlefields/.

Adolphus, Frederick. "Basics about Confederate Uniforms." Adolphus Confederate Uniforms. Updated December 21, 2020. http://adolphusconfederateuniforms.com/basics-of-confederate-uniforms.html.

African American Surname Matches from 1870. "Jefferson County." RootsWeb. Accessed January 20, 2023. https://sites.rootsweb.com/~ajac/msjefferson.htm.

American Battlefield Trust. "The Battle of Thompson's Station." March 26, 2021. https://www.battlefields.org/learn/civil-war/battles/thompsons-station.

The American Civil War. "The Battle of Farmington." Accessed January 19, 2023. http://www.americancivilwar101.com/battles/620509-farmington.html.

———. "Earl Van Dorn." Accessed January 19, 2023. https://www.battlefields.org/learn/biographies/earl-van-dorn.

———. "Fort Sumter." Accessed January 20, 2023. https://www.battlefields.org/learn/civil-war/battles/fort-sumter.

————. "Gen. P.G.T. Beauregard to Maj. Robert Anderson." Accessed January 20, 2023. https://www.battlefields.org/learn/primary-sources/gen-p-g-t-beauregard-maj-robert-anderson.

————. "Iuka." Accessed January 19, 2023. https://www.battlefields.org/learn/civil-war/battles/iuka.

————. "Pea Ridge." Accessed January 19, 2023. https://www.battlefields.org/learn/civil-war/battles/pea-ridge.

————. "Pensacola (1814)." Accessed January 17, 2023. https://www.battlefields.org/learn/war-1812/battles/pensacola.

————. "William J. Hardee." https://www.battlefields.org/learn/biographies/william-j-hardee.

Andrews, Evan. "The Amazonian Expedition That Nearly Killed Theodore Roosevelt." History.com. Updated September 4, 2018. https://www.history.com/news/the-amazonian-expedition-that-nearly-killed-theodore-roosevelt.

Army Heritage Center Foundation. "Answering the Call: The Personal Equipment of a Civil War Soldier." Accessed January 19, 2023. https://www.armyheritage.org/soldier-stories-information/answering-the-call-the-personal-equipment-of-a-civil-war-soldier/.

Bamberg (SC) Herald. November 20, 1902. Library of Congress. https://www.loc.gov/item/sn86063790/1902-11-20/ed-1/.

Barber, Rhett. "Holt Collier." Dixie Outfitters. March 25, 2017. https://dixieoutfitters.com/2015/04/04/holt-collier/.

Baxter Springs (KS) News. April 12, 1902. Library of Congress. https://www.loc.gov/item/sn83040592/1902-04-12/ed-1/.

Bear Education and Restoration Group (BEaR). "Bear Info." Accessed January 17, 2023. https://msbear.org/bear-info/.

Biography.com. "William McKinley." Updated May 5, 2021. https://www.biography.com/us-president/william-mckinley.

Bomboy, Scott. "On This Day, Theodore Roosevelt Dies Unexpectedly." National Constitution Center. January 6, 2023. https://constitutioncenter.org/blog/what-if-another-roosevelt-were-on-the-1920-presidential-ballot.

Bradley, Michael R. "Nathan Bedford Forrest." Essential Civil War Curriculum. Accessed January 19, 2023. https://www.essentialcivilwarcurriculum.com/nathan-bedford-forrest.html.

Brewminate. "Gambling on the Frontier in 19th-Century America." December 17, 2020. https://brewminate.com/gambling-on-the-frontier-in-19th-century-america/.

Bridges, Ken. "Texas History Minute: The Story of Lawrence Sullivan 'Sul' Ross." *Weatherford Democrat*, August 7, 2021. https://www. weatherforddemocrat.com/opinion/columns/texas-history-minute-the-story-of-lawrence-sullivan-sul-ross/article_075797e4-072a-5ed6-a050-37abab5e2856.html.

Brinkley, Douglas. *The Wilderness Warrior: Theodore Roosevelt and the Crusade for America*. New York: Harper Collins, 2009.

Brune, Herman W. "Legend, Lore & Legacy: Ben Lilly." *Texas Parks & Wildlife* (January 2003). https://tpwmagazine.com/archive/2003/jan/legend/.

Buchanan, Minor Ferris. *Holt Collier: His Life, His Roosevelt Hunts, and the Origin of the Teddy Bear*. Jackson, MS: Centennial Press, 2002.

Bullock Museum. "African Americans." Accessed January 19, 2023. https://www.thestoryoftexas.com/discover/campfire-stories/african-americans.

Bunn, J. Michael, and Clay Williams. "Mississippi's Territorial Years: A Momentous and Contentious Affair (1798–1817)." Mississippi History Now. November 2008. https://www.mshistorynow.mdah.ms.gov/issue/mississippis-territorial-years-1798-1817.

Calberg, A.M. "19th Century Riverboats Gambling, Mississippi." Historical Fiction Writers Research Blog. January 26, 2012. https://ladyamcal.wordpress.com/2012/01/25/19th-century-riverboats-gambling-mississippi/.

The Canebrake Hall of Fame. Accessed January 19, 2023. http://canebrakes.com/halloffame.html.

Carlos, Ann M. "The Economic History of the Fur Trade: 1670 to 1870." EH.net. Accessed January 19, 2023. https://eh.net/encyclopedia/the-economic-history-of-the-fur-trade-1670-to-1870/.

Carter, Samuel. *The Last Cavaliers: Confederate and Union Cavalry in the Civil War*. New York: St. Martin's Press, 1979.

Catton, Bruce. "Grant at Shiloh." *American Heritage* 11, no. 2 (February 1960). https://www.americanheritage.com/grant-shiloh.

Civil War and Reconstruction Governors of Mississippi. "Plantations— Home Hill Plantation (Natchez, Miss.)" Accessed January 20, 2023. https://cwrgm.org/item/S25023807.

The Civil War in Missouri. "General Sterling Price." Accessed January 19, 2023. http://civilwarmo.org/educators/resources/info-sheets/general-sterling-price.

CivilWarTalk. Accessed January 20, 2023. https://civilwartalk.com/.

Crump, Louise Eskrigge. "History." The Official Website of Greenville Mississippi. Accessed January 18, 2023. https://greenvillems.org/history/.

Cunningham, Edward, Gary D. Joiner and Timothy B. Smith. *Shiloh and the Western Campaign of 1862*. New York: Savas Beatie, 2012.

Cunningham, John M. "United States Presidential Election of 1904." Encyclopædia Britannica. Last updated November 1, 2022. https://www.britannica.com/event/United-States-presidential-election-of-1904.

Daniel, Larry J. *Shiloh: The Battle That Changed the Civil War*. Norwalk, CT: Easton Press, 2004.

Dobie, J. Frank. "Mister Ben Lilly in Louisiana." *Southwest Review* 29, no. 2 (Winter 1944): 215–33.

Encyclopædia Britannica. "Albert Sidney Johnston." Last updated April 2, 2023. https://www.britannica.com/biography/Albert-Sidney-Johnston.
———. "Bull Moose Party." Revised and expanded July 15, 2015. https://www.britannica.com/topic/Bull-Moose-Party.

Encyclopedia of Alabama. "Inauguration of Jefferson Davis." Accessed January 17, 2023. http://encyclopediaofalabama.org/article/m-3598.

Evening Star (Washington, D.C.). December 9, 1907. Library of Congress. https://www.loc.gov/item/sn83045462/1907-12-09/ed-1/.
———. November 21, 1902. Library of Congress. https://www.loc.gov/item/sn83045462/1902-11-21/ed-1/.
———. October 13, 1907. Library of Congress. https://www.loc.gov/item/sn83045462/1907-10-13/ed-1/.

Facing History & Ourselves. "Statistics from the Civil War." Last updated August 12, 2022. https://www.facinghistory.org/resource-library/statistics-civil-war.

Farm Progress. "Teddy Roosevelt Relished Bear Hunt in Louisiana." August 3, 2007. https://www.farmprogress.com/management/teddy-roosevelt-relished-bear-hunt-in-louisiana.

Fickle, James E. "Forests and Forest Products before 1930." Mississippi Encyclopedia. Center for Study of Southern Culture. April 14, 2018. https://mississippiencyclopedia.org/entries/forests-and-forest-products-before-1930/.

F.M. Allen Camp Smoke (blog). "The Forgotten Legend of Holt Collier." September 9, 2009. https://campsmoke.wordpress.com/2009/09/09/the-forgotten-legend-of-holt-collier/.

Foner, Eric. *Reconstruction: America's Unfinished Revolution, 1863–1877*. New York: Harper Perennial Modern Classics, 2014.

Forbes, John. "Capture of Jeff Davis." Mississippi State University Scholars Junction, Frank and Virginia Williams Collection of Lincolniana. Originally published 1865. https://scholarsjunction.msstate.edu/cgi/viewcontent.cgi?article=1591&context=fvw-pamphlets.

The Gilder Lehrman Institute of American History. "De Soto's Discovery of the Mississippi, 1541." Accessed January 20, 2023. https://www.gilderlehrman.org/history-resources/spotlight-primary-source/de-sotos-discovery-mississippi-1541.

Giles, Mike. "Holt Collier and the Teddy Bear." *Meridian Star*, July 8, 2016. https://www.meridianstar.com/sports/holt-collier-and-the-teddy-bear/article_cdee6dcc-44aa-11e6-8144-a7afd599cec8.html.

Hall, John C. "Canebrakes." Encyclopedia of Alabama. Last updated March 27, 2023. http://encyclopediaofalabama.org/ARTICLE/h-1279.

Hess, Earl J., and Brendan Wolfe. "Pickett's Charge." Encyclopedia Virginia, February 12, 2021. https://encyclopediavirginia.org/entries/picketts-charge/.

The Historical Marker Database. "The Story of Teddy Bears." October 10, 2020. https://www.hmdb.org/m.asp?m=157613.

History.com Editors. "Battle of Corinth." History.com. Updated August 21, 2018. https://www.history.com/topics/american-civil-war/battle-of-corinth.

———. "Jim Crow Laws." History.com. Updated April 11, 2023. https://www.history.com/topics/early-20th-century-us/jim-crow-laws.

———. "Secession." History.com. Updated June 7, 2019. https://www.history.com/topics/american-civil-war/secession.

———. "Sharecropping." History.com. Updated March 29, 2023. https://www.history.com/topics/black-history/sharecropping.

———. "War of 1812." History.com. Updated: April 24, 2023. https://www.history.com/topics/19th-century/war-of-1812.

History.com. "Jefferson Davis Elected Confederate President." November 13, 2009. https://www.history.com/this-day-in-history/jefferson-davis-elected-confederate-president.

———. "Robert E. Lee Surrenders." November 24, 2009. https://www.history.com/this-day-in-history/robert-e-lee-surrenders.

———. "Theodore Roosevelt Shot in Milwaukee." February 9, 2010. https://www.history.com/this-day-in-history/theodore-roosevelt-shot-in-milwaukee.

————. "Theodore Roosevelt's Wife and Mother Die." November 16, 2009. https://www.history.com/this-day-in-history/theodore-roosevelts-wife-and-mother-die.

Hollandsworth, James G., Jr. "Black Confederate Pensioners after the Civil War." Mississippi History Now. May 2008. https://www.mshistorynow.mdah.ms.gov/issue/black-confederate-pensioners-after-the-civil-war.

Holly Springs, NC, Official Website. "The Civil War in Holly Springs." Accessed January 19, 2023. https://www.hollyspringsnc.us/379/The-Civil-War-in-Holly-Springs.

Hoover, Jeff "Tank." "The Legend of Ben Lilly." American Handgunner, August 7, 2020. https://americanhandgunner.com/discover/the-legend-of-ben-lilly/.

Humanities Texas. "Cynthia Ann Parker." https://www.humanitiestexas.org/programs/tx-originals/list/cynthia-ann-parker.

Jeffers, H. Paul. Colonel Roosevelt: Theodore Roosevelt Goes to War, 1897–1898. New York: J. Wiley & Sons, 1996.

Jefferson County. "The Jefferson Flying Artillery Also Known as Harper's Battery and Later as Darden's Battery." Accessed January 20, 2023. https://www.msgw.org/jefferson/military/jeffflyingartillery.html.

Jewish Virtual Library: A Project of American-Israeli Cooperative Enterprise (AICE). "Rose & Morris Michtom (1870–1938)." Accessed January 19, 2023. https://www.jewishvirtuallibrary.org/rose-and-morris-michtom.

Johnson, Walter. River of Dark Dreams Slavery and Empire in the Cotton Kingdom. Cambridge, MA: Belknap Press of Harvard University Press, 2017.

Knapp, Charles. "Hogs Roman and Modern Boar Hunting, Ancient and Modern." Classical Weekly 28, no. 11 (1935): 81. https://doi.org/10.2307/4339472.

Lea, Henry Charles. "The Record of the Democratic Party, 1860–1865." Mississippi State University Scholars Junction, Frank and Virginia Williams Collection of Lincolniana. Originally published 1865. https://scholarsjunction.msstate.edu/cgi/viewcontent.cgi?article=1868&context=fvw-pamphlets.

Legends of America. "Ben Lilly: Bears, Blades & Contradictions." Accessed January 19, 2023. https://www.legendsofamerica.com/we-benlilly/.

Levin, Kevin M. "Does This Mean No More Talk of Black Confederates?" October 18, 2011. http://cwmemory.com/2010/05/24/does-this-mean-no-more-talk-of-black-confederates/.

Lincoln, Abraham. "Lincoln's Inaugural and First Message to Congress." Mississippi State University Scholars Junction, Frank and Virginia Williams Collection of Lincolniana. Originally published 1894. https://scholarsjunction.msstate.edu/cgi/viewcontent.cgi?article=1227&context=fvw-pamphlets.

McDevitt, David. "Lucius Wing's Big Adventure in Holly Springs." Ohio History Connection. May 16, 2022. https://www.ohiohistory.org/lucius-wings-big-adventure-in-holly-springs/.

Mississippi Department of Archives and History "Winterville Mounds." Accessed January 20, 2023. https://www.mdah.ms.gov/explore-mississippi/winterville-mounds.

Mississippi Department of Corrections. "A Brief History of the Mississippi Department of Corrections." Accessed January 17, 2023. https://www.mdoc.ms.gov/About/Pages/Brief-History.aspx.

Mississippi Department of Wildlife, Fisheries and Parks. "Black Bear Program." Accessed January 18, 2023. https://www.mdwfp.com/wildlife-hunting/black-bear-program/.

Mississippi Encyclopedia. "Issaquena County." April 14, 2018. https://mississippiencyclopedia.org/entries/issaquena-county/.

———. "Sharkey County." April 15, 2018. https://mississippiencyclopedia.org/entries/sharkey-county/.

———. "Washington County." April 15, 2018. https://mississippiencyclopedia.org/entries/washington-county/.

Mississippi History Now. "The Mississippi Constitution of 1890 as Originally Adopted." Accessed January 20, 2023. https://www.mshistorynow.mdah.ms.gov/issue/mississippi-constitution-of-1890-as-originally-adopted.

Mississippi History Timeline. "1519–1797 » 1779-1797, Spanish Dominion." Accessed January 20, 2023. http://timeline.mdah.ms.gov/zone/1779-1797-spanish-dominion/.

Mississippi's Lower Delta Partnership. "The Amazing Holt Collier: Mississippi's Famous Hunting Guide." July 3, 2019. https://www.lowerdelta.org/community-news/the-amazing-holt-collier-mississippis-famous-hunting-guide/.

Momodu, Samuel. "Black Cowboys in the 19th Century West (1850-1900)." BlackPast. February 18, 2022. https://www.blackpast.org/african-american-history/concepts-african-american-history/black-cowboys-in-the-19th-century-west-1850-1900/.

Moncrief, Robert L. "When Teddy Roosevelt Went Bear Hunting in Louisiana." Madison Parish, Louisiana Historical and Genealogical Data. Accessed January 18, 2023. https://sites.rootsweb.com/~lamadiso/articles/roosevelt_moncrief.htm.

Monish. "Holt Collier American Big Game Hunter." AfricaHunting.com. July 26, 2010. https://www.africahunting.com/threads/holt-collier-american-big-game-hunter.15076/.

Moore, Sandra Guthrie. "Hunters in & around Carroll Parish." East Carroll Parish, Louisiana Genealogy. October 9, 2009. http://eastcarrollparishlouisianagenealogy.blogspot.com/2009/10/people-in-around-carroll-parish.html.

Mote, Nathan. "The Forgotten Legend of Holt Collier." The Heritage Post. December 30, 2020. https://heritagepost.org/american-civil-war/the-forgotten-legend-of-holt-collier/.

Murphy, Libby. "Battle of Shiloh Interrupted Breakfast." *Jackson Sun*, April 6, 2016. https://www.jacksonsun.com/story/life/food/2016/04/05/battle-shiloh-interrupted-breakfast-cherry-mansion/82686694/.

Nast, Thomas, Alfred R. Waud, Henry L. Stephens, James E. Taylor, J. Hoover, George F. Crane and Elizabeth White. "The African American Odyssey: A Quest for Full Citizenship: Reconstruction and Its Aftermath." Library of Congress. February 9, 1998. https://www.loc.gov/exhibits/african-american-odyssey/reconstruction.html.

Natchez (MS) Democrat. "About Those Black Confederates..." March 7, 2018. https://www.natchezdemocrat.com/2018/03/07/about-those-black-confederates/.

National Endowment for the Humanities. "The Canton Times. (Canton, Miss.) 1893–1906, November 21, 1902, Image 3." News about Chronicling America RSS. M.L. Dinkins.

———. "The Caucasian. (Shreveport, La.) 1900–192?, October 22, 1907, Image 2." News about Chronicling America RSS. Caucasian Pub. Co. Accessed January 18, 2023.

———. "The Greenville Times. [Volume] (Greenville, Miss.) 1868–1917, August 25, 1877, Image 3." News about Chronicling America RSS. Publisher not identified. Accessed January 19, 2023.

———. "The Greenville Times. [Volume] (Greenville, Miss.) 1868–1917, November 26, 1904, Image 10." News about Chronicling America RSS. Publisher not identified. Accessed January 19, 2023.

———. "The Grenada Sentinel. [Volume] (Grenada, Miss.) 1868–1955, October 19, 1907, Image 7." News about Chronicling America RSS. John N. Bowen & Co. Accessed January 18, 2023.

———. "Hattiesburg Daily News. (Hattiesburg, Miss.) 1907–1908, October 22, 1907, Image 1." News about Chronicling America RSS. Hattiesburg Print. & Pub. Co. Accessed January 18, 2023.

———. "Sistersville Daily Oil Review. [Volume] (Sistersville, W. Va.) 1902–1905, November 15, 1902, Image 1." News about Chronicling America RSS. J.H. McCoy. Accessed January 18, 2023.

National Geographic Society. "Apr 7, 1862 CE: Battle of Shiloh." Accessed January 20, 2023. https://education.nationalgeographic.org/resource/battle-shiloh.

National Park Planner. "Shiloh National Military Park: Corinth Unit: Confederate Siege Lines." February 3, 2022. https://npplan.com/parks-by-state/tennessee/shiloh-national-military-park-park-at-a-glance/shiloh-national-military-park-corinth-unit/shiloh-national-military-park-corinth-unit-confederate-siege-lines/.

National Park Service. "The Bull Moose in Winter: Theodore Roosevelt and World War I." Accessed January 18, 2023. https://www.nps.gov/articles/the-bull-moose-in-winter-theodore-roosevelt-and-world-war-i.htm.

New-York Tribune. January 3, 1907. Library of Congress. https://www.loc.gov/item/sn83030214/1907-01-03/ed-1/.

———. June 7, 1907. Library of Congress. https://www.loc.gov/item/sn83030214/1907-06-07/ed-1/.

———. March 26, 1907. Library of Congress. https://www.loc.gov/item/sn83030214/1907-03-26/ed-1/.

Nicholas, R. Nelson. "Ninth Texas Cavalry." Texas State Historical Association. Updated June 9, 2011. https://www.tshaonline.org/handbook/entries/ninth-texas-cavalry.

Nordberg, Ken. "How to Properly Field Dress a Bear." Dr. Ken Nordberg's Article Archive. First printed in Bear Hunting Magazine, March/April 2002. https://www.drnordbergondeerhunting.com/hypertext/Articles/Field_Dress_a_Bear.html.

Nowell, Princella Wilkerson. "The Flood of 1927 and Its Impact in Greenville, Mississippi." Mississippi History Now. March 2006. https://www.mshistorynow.mdah.ms.gov/issue/the-flood-of-1927-and-its-impact-in-greenville-mississippi.

O'Brian, Bill. "Theodore Roosevelt & the Teddy Bear." U.S. Fish & Wildlife Service. June 30, 2022. https://www.fws.gov/story/theodore-roosevelt-teddy-bear.

Ouchley, Kelby. "Teddy Roosevelt's Bear Hunt." 64 Parishes. Last updated April 29, 2019. https://64parishes.org/entry/teddy-roosevelts-bear-hunt.

PBS. "The Civil War by the Numbers." Accessed January 19, 2023. https://www.pbs.org/wgbh/americanexperience/features/death-numbers/.

————. "Greenville, Mississippi Rejects the Ku Klux Klan." Accessed January 18, 2023. https://www.pbs.org/wgbh/americanexperience/features/flood-greenville/.

————. "Sharecropping." Accessed January 19, 2023. https://www.pbs.org/tpt/slavery-by-another-name/themes/sharecropping/.

peashooter85. "Holt Collier—Black Confederate and Bear Killer." Lock, Stock, and History. Tumblr. January 18, 2016. https://www.tumblr.com/peashooter85/137520295055/holt-collier-black-confederate-and-bear-killer.

Phillips, Gene. "Washington County Biographies." Genealogy Trails History Group. Accessed January 19, 2023. http://genealogytrails.com/miss/washington/bios.html.

Phillips, Jason. "Reconstruction." Mississippi Encyclopedia. April 15, 2018. https://mississippiencyclopedia.org/entries/reconstruction/.

Renehan, Edward J. *The Lion's Pride: Theodore Roosevelt and His Family in Peace and War.* New York: Oxford University Press, 2000.

Rhodes College Archives and Special Collections. "The Bear Hunt of 1902." Accessed January 19, 2023. http://archives.rhodes.edu/exhibits/show/footeparkways/foote_bear_1903.

Roosevelt, Theodore. "In the Louisiana Canebrakes." *Scribner's Magazine* 43, no. 1 (January 1908): 47–60. Madison Parish, Louisiana Historical and Genealogical Data. Accessed January 19, 2023. https://sites.rootsweb.com/~lamadiso/articles/louisianacanebrakes.htm.

Russell, Ramsey. "Holt Collier, Legendary Mississippi Bear Hunter (Part 2)." *Duck Season Somewhere* podcast, November 23, 2020. https://www.getducks.com/duckseasonsomewhere/holt-collier-legendary-mississippi-bear-hunter/.

Samway, Patrick H. "The Birmingham Years." *New York Times.* 1997. https://archive.nytimes.com/www.nytimes.com/books/first/s/samway-percy.html.

Shapell Manuscript Foundation. "Vice President Theodore Roosevelt, On Hearing That McKinley Has Been Shot, Wires for News." January 17, 2018. https://www.shapell.org/manuscript/tr-mckinley-assassination/.

Shur, Robert Collins. "The Road to Corinth." American Battlefield Trust. October 11, 2022. https://www.battlefields.org/learn/articles/battle-corinth.

Simek, Stephanie L., Jerrold L. Belant, Brad W. Young, Catherine Shropshire and Bruce D. Leopold. "History and Status of the American Black Bear in Mississippi." *Ursus* 23, no. 2 (2012): 159–67. https://doi.org/10.2192/ursus-d-11-00031.1.

Somerville, Lucy. "The Mississippi Flood of 1927." Mississippi History Now. As published in the June 1927 edition of *Woman's Press*. https://www.mshistorynow.mdah.ms.gov/issue/the-mississippi-flood-of-1927.

The Strong National Museum of Play "Teddy Bear." November 10, 2021. https://www.museumofplay.org/toys/teddy-bear/.

The Sun (New York, NY). December 6, 1907. Library of Congress. https://www.loc.gov/item/sn83030272/1907-12-06/ed-1/.

———. October 1, 1897. Library of Congress. https://www.loc.gov/item/sn83030272/1897-10-01/ed-1/.

Taylor, Amy Murrell. "Texts and Textiles in Civil War Kentucky." *Register of the Kentucky Historical Society* 117, no. 2 (2019): 229–44. https://doi.org/10.1353/khs.2019.0061.

Theodore Roosevelt Center. "Letter from Theodore Roosevelt to Holt Collier." December 24, 1907. https://www.theodorerooseveltcenter.org/Research/Digital-Library/Record/ImageViewer?libID=o201056.

Theodore Roosevelt Inaugural Site. "The Inauguration." Accessed January 19, 2023. https://www.trsite.org/learn/the-day-of-the-inauguration.

Thompson, Kathleen. "When Did Slavery Really End in the North?" Civil Discourse. January 9, 2017. http://civildiscourse-historyblog.com/blog/2017/1/3/when-did-slavery-really-end-in-the-north.

Topeka (KS) State Journal. December 11, 1902. Library of Congress. https://www.loc.gov/item/sn82016014/1902-12-11/ed-1/.

———. December 9, 1902. https://www.loc.gov/resource/sn82016014/1902-12-09/ed-1/.

———. October 12, 1907. Library of Congress. https://www.loc.gov/resource/sn82016014/1907-10-12/ed-1/.

Washington (D.C.) Herald. June 23, 1907. Accessed January 19, 2023. https://www.loc.gov/resource/sn83045433/1907-06-23/ed-1/.

———. October 27, 1907. Library of Congress. https://www.loc.gov/item/sn83045433/1907-10-27/ed-1/.

Welch, Frank J. "The Plantation Land Tenure System in Mississippi." Mississippi State University Scholars Junction, MAFES Technical Bulletins. Originally published 1943. https://scholarsjunction.msstate.edu/cgi/viewcontent.cgi?article=1019&context=mafes-tech-bulletins.

The White House. "Theodore Roosevelt." December 23, 2022. https://www.whitehouse.gov/about-the-white-house/presidents/theodore-roosevelt/.

WikiTree. "John Hinds (1753–1807)." Last modified August 11, 2021. https://www.wikitree.com/wiki/Hinds-604.

———. "Thomas Marston Green Sr. (1723–1805)." December 2, 2022. https://www.wikitree.com/wiki/Green-12842.

Wills, Brian Steel. *A Battle from the Start: The Life of Nathan Bedford Forrest.* New York: HarperPerennial, 1993.

Winchester Repeating Arms. "Model 1886 Lever-Action Rifles." Accessed January 18, 2023. https://www.winchesterguns.com/products/rifles/model-1886.html.

The World of 1898: The Spanish-American War (Hispanic Division, Library of Congress). "Rough Riders." Accessed January 19, 2023. https://loc.gov/rr/hispanic/1898/roughriders.html.

Young, Brad. "Black Bears in Mississippi, Past and Present." Mississippi Department of Wildlife, Fisheries, and Parks. Accessed January 19, 2023. https://www.mdwfp.com/wildlife-hunting/black-bear-program/black-bears-in-ms.aspx.

Young, Brad W. "Black Bears." Mississippi Encyclopedia. April 13, 2018. https://mississippiencyclopedia.org/entries/black-bears/.

ABOUT THE AUTHOR

Courtesy of Icon Studio Portrait Design, Tupelo, MS.

Mark Neaves is a lifelong resident of northeast Mississippi. He has spent over twenty years teaching history in Mississippi public schools and at the community college level. Mark graduated from Mississippi University for Women in 1999 with a bachelor's degree in social studies education. He also holds a master's degree in secondary education from the University of Mississippi and a master's in ministry from Heritage Christian University. Mark is married to Marti Neaves, his wife of twenty-two years, and they have two children, Riley and Emma Kay. He is currently teaching American History 2 at a Mississippi public high school. He also coauthored the book *Little Fish, Big Splash*. He hopes to continue writing history books in the future.

Visit us at
www.historypress.com